I0441219

Prepping for Beginners
A Collection of 4 Survival Books

By Robert Paine

© 2014

All rights reserved. No part of this publication may be reproduced, distributed, or transmitted in any form or by any means, including photocopying, recording, or other electronic or mechanical methods, without the prior written permission of the publisher, except in the case of brief quotations embodied in critical reviews and certain other noncommercial uses permitted by copyright law.

Are You and Your Family Ready to Survive the Next Disaster?

If you have ever thought about prepping, you have probably been a bit overwhelmed, at least once or twice. It can seem like a monumental task that will take too much work. Where do you start?

You have to start somewhere. You can start with this collection of 4 best-selling prepping guides. With Prepping for Beginners: A Collection of 4 Survival Books, you'll get:

10 Ways to Start Prepping Today
Top 10 Prepping Mistakes (and How to Avoid Them)
Bug Out Bag Basics
The Grid Down Prepper: How to survive when the power goes out

If you are interested in learning how to protect your family from any and all of the inevitable disasters that could potentially happen, this book collection is your first step to learning how to prepare for any emergency situation.

Survivors are a unique group of people. Some people call us Survivalists, Doomsday Preppers, or Patriots. You may not consider yourself any of those things. Whatever you may want to call yourself, if you're reading this, you are on the first step to helping your family survive, no matter what.

So grab Prepping for Beginners: A Collection of 4 Survival Books today and get all 4 best-selling Prepper books and always be prepared!

Sign up for Robert's Mailing List to be notified of **New Releases**

and **Special Sales**: http://eepurl.com/zvm11

10 Ways to Start Prepping Today

If you have ever thought about prepping, you have probably been a bit overwhelmed, at least once or twice. It can seem like a monumental task that will take too much work. Where do you start? You see these pictures of food storage shelters or pantries that have enough food to last a family a year or more and it can be daunting. Maybe you have read stories of people creating these bunkers or hideouts in the woods with a huge cache of emergency supplies. You are probably thinking, "That will take me forever! I don't even know where to begin." Well, like a wise man once said a few hundred years ago, "Rome wasn't built in a day," and neither are those vast emergency food storages.

You have to start somewhere. Somewhere small. Somewhere easy. You can start with these ten things, today. It isn't all about buying food and supplies. There is a lot of research and planning that goes into prepping. That is going to be where your prepping journey starts. Grab a pen and paper and prepare to write down the thoughts that pop into your head as you read along. Remember, your prepping is best done in manageable, bite-size pieces. It will be less overwhelming and you won't feel like you are trying to climb a mountain. Slow and easy is the way to go!

1) Research and Educate Yourself About Prepping.

Fairly obvious for a first step, no? Still, you'd be surprised how many so-called Preppers have never even read anything on the subject! Yes, it sounds tedious, but you are going to discover there is a plethora of information available about prepping, everywhere you look. Books, movies, TV shows, podcasts, and on and on. Some of it is helpful while some of it is really quite pointless and a waste of time. You need information that will prove of some value to you. Prepping is an activity that requires careful consideration. Every family and every individual will have different needs. When you are looking for materials about prepping, follow those that offer real solutions and suggestions that you can apply to your family. If something doesn't apply to you and your situation, skip it. If you live in the city, look for prepping materials geared toward the urban prepper. Reading about raising cattle and farming isn't going to be of much use to you if you plan on living in your high-rise apartment in the middle of the city.

Ebooks (like mine! And many others!) are great for finding information quickly. However, you will want to have print copies of the research you uncover as much as possible. What are you gonna do if the grid goes down?! Part of prepping is preparing to deal with long term power outages, which means your Kindle or Nook isn't going to work so well. All that beautiful information will be out of reach. Now is the time to really get organized. It is a good idea to keep all your research in a binder. Take the time to keep it all straight, with tabs and everything else you can think of. This will make it easy for you to quickly flip to the information you need when you are in a rush. A binder is a great way to keep all your research together in one place. Your family will also be able to find what they need in case you are not immediately available. Keep your binder with your emergency preps for easy access.

Don't stop at just one resource. You will discover there are a lot of really good ideas out there. Nobody preps the same. Some ideas will work for you and your family, while some will not. Learn from other people's mistakes. There is no need to reinvent the wheel. Again, I know it may seem really obvious, but don't skip this vital first part of prepping: Do your research and educate yourself!

2) Create, Study, and Practice your Overall Emergency Plan (and then do it all again!)

You know those little maps on the back of hotel room doors that indicate where you are in the building? The maps have a red line that indicates the path for you to escape in case of an emergency. Those maps are there for a reason. When there is a situation that threatens your life and that of your family, you tend to get a little crazy. You could end up running in circles because you are panicking. Prepping eliminates those little panic attacks that threaten your life and sends you running in circles.

You need an emergency plan for your family. A map, of sorts, that tells you all what steps you're going to take in case of an emergency. This is going to require you to think of all the little details that are likely to arise in a true emergency. All of the things that you will be too busy to think about when the situation actually arises. Now is the time to think about them and to plan for them.

Brainstorm different plans and write them down. Put them away for an hour and come back to them and review your different strategies. Do you see any flaws or pieces of the puzzle missing? For example, if you are going to be hunkering down in your basement, who is going to ensure the front door is locked and barricaded? Who is going to make sure each of the children in the family gets to the basement safely? What are you going to do with your pets? Who will be in charge of doing a head count? Does the entire family know they are supposed to get to the basement when you give the word?

Pick each member of your family's brains for their best ideas. You cannot do it all and you don't want to do it alone. Get everyone in your household involved. The more people you have, the more chances you have to catch important things that you may have missed if you are trying to do it all alone. You need to rely on every source available. Once you have come up with what you think is a pretty good emergency plan, do a run through. Practice and drill it as though the event is actually taking place. Everyone needs to approach this with a serious mindset. This is going to be a bit rough the first few times through – that's okay. Expect the family to be running in circles the first couple of times you test out your plan. Each time should get a little easier and a little more orderly. This is what you are trying to achieve. Practice makes perfect! That perfect plan you put together is going to have holes in it when you actually put it into action. This is why you are drilling it.

You absolutely must physically practice your emergency plan. This is the only way to discover those little hiccups in the plan.

Time yourself and the family. How long does it take to get everybody into the basement? Are there things you can do to make the retreat go a little smoother and faster? Once you have established a plan, you will want to practice at least once a month to keep everybody familiar with it. If you move a piece of furniture or add a new member to the family, you need to tweak your plan. Try practicing for different scenarios. If the grid goes down and there is no power, how will your reactions be different? If there is a flood and water is in the basement, making it unusable, where will you go as a backup? The more scenarios you practice and prepare for, the better off everyone in the family will be. You will feel confident that everyone will know what to do, regardless of the reason that the plan needs to be put into place. And really, isn't that what prepping is all about?

3) Create a Bug Out Bag (BOB)

Your next step is to start putting together a bug out bag, or at least deciding what you need to start gathering to put in your bug out bag. A bug out bag is essentially a backpack or duffel filled with tools you would need to survive out in the open. Typically, the bag should be filled with items that will keep you alive as you travel from point A to point B or if you are stranded somewhere. A 3-day supply of food (and water, if possible) is typical for a bug out bag. The bags are not meant to sustain an entire family for a full month, but each bag should support one person for up to 72 hours.

Bug out bags must be fairly lightweight so they don't hinder you. You need to be able to move freely, quickly, and easily while carrying your BOB. A bag that is loaded with everything but the kitchen sink is like an albatross around your neck and could actually put your life in jeopardy. You cannot maneuver quickly when you are carrying around 100 pounds of gear. It could slow you down, cause you to trip and fall or strain your back. All of which are extremely serious and potentially life-threatening in a survival situation.

Do some research on the various types of bags that can be used as a bug out bag. A framed backpack is ideal for packing the most gear. Look for them at camping stores or hiking outlets. General sporting goods stores may also carry them. However, the downside is that these packs tend to be rather expensive. If you can swing it or find one that is on sale or possibly used, definitely go for it. Their design makes them hands down the best choice for a BOB. The internal frame helps distribute the weight of the pack across your hips and shoulders. They tend to be way more comfortable to pack around. If you think your situation will call for you to hike several miles, or if you live anywhere that isn't flat, with some hills or even mountains, you should consider investing in one of these packs.

If you can't find, can't afford, or simply don't want a hiking pack, then a standard backpack will suffice. However, you will want to find one that has the hip belt and pads. It may not seem like much when you try it on at the store, but when you are walking several miles with a pack weighing more than 30 pounds, you will appreciate the extra padding and support on your hips and lower back. You will also want to look for a bag that has plenty of internal and external pockets. This will help keep your gear organized. Places to clip gear to the outside of the pack is also essential. You want to have easy access to things like a whistle and flashlight or knife. Clipping them outside your pack makes them quick and easy to grab when the situation demands it. You don't want to have to stop, open the pack, and fumble around for something that you may need in a split second.

Usually it's safe to say: Don't waste your time with duffel bags, suitcases or other bags that require you to use your hands to carry them. They are much more trouble than they are worth. You will offset your center of gravity and struggle to walk. You will need to stop anytime you want to get something out of the bag. They're often awkward or cumbersome to move quickly with, or to scale any sort of terrain. You will need your hands free to carry a flashlight or other tools, and these types of bags simply don't allow for those situations easily enough.

So, you got your bag picked out – now what? Now you need to figure out what you're going to load it up with! At a minimum, your bug out bag should include the following;

- Matches, flint steel, or lighter
- Flashlight
- Whistle
- Energy bars
- Basic first aid kit

- Emergency blanket
- Cordage i.e. paracord
- Canteen
- Water purification tablets and perhaps one or two bottles of water
- Knife
- Another weapon is optional. A can of Mace, pepper spray or a taser are all great, cheap options if you are not comfortable carrying a gun.

Those are some of the very basic items you will need. Of course, it's not a complete list of everything you may need or want – that will be very situation-dependent. You will want to tweak your bug out bag to suit your needs and the climate you live in. Rain gear, extra socks, a hat and gloves are all options. Have some options for winter as well, if you live somewhere that this will be an issue. You don't want to pack the perfect bug out bag, only to find out that you have to use it in the middle of December and, whoops, you didn't pack any winter gear!

If you require prescription medications include a supply of your medicines in the bag. If you have a serious allergy, buy an extra Epi-Pen to keep in your bug out bag. Each member of the family should have a bug out bag. Children's bug out bags will obviously be much smaller, but they should have some of the basic gear just in case they get separated from you. Make sure you choose a backpack that is the right size for your child. Adult packs are not suitable for a child's small size. Having a child help brainstorm what they should pack, picking out the perfect bag for them, and having them help pack it up nice and tight, is a great way to get children involved and help them feel like they are really an important part of the process (because, they are!). Giving them some control over their bug out bag will really help cement this in their minds.

4) Choose Your Locations (Main, Backup, and Backup for the Backup!)

Part of prepping is always having a backup plan. And then having a backup to your backup. You cannot predict what will happen or how it will affect you. You can, however, prepare for almost anything. That old saying, "Prepare for the worst and hope for the best," applies to prepping. You hope you won't have to leave the comfort of your house with all of your things, but there is a real possibility you will have to leave it all behind. You need a rally point, so to speak, for your family to retreat to if your home is compromised. A meet up place. Somewhere that everyone will remember in any time of crisis.

Many preppers living in the city choose to have a location somewhere outside of town to retreat to. That's fine, if you're able to get out of town, once something goes bad. Have a backup plan for another location in the city, if all exits are blocked. Ideally, you want somewhere that is close enough for you to walk to if necessary, but far enough out of the city (or hidden enough inside of the city) that you won't have to worry about dealing with too many unscrupulous people trying to get to your emergency food supply or any other of your items. This is where you will store the majority of your emergency supplies. The bug out bag we talked about in the last section is what will sustain you on your journey to reach the second location.

If you already live outside of town, you will probably still need to have a second location picked out. Maybe you live in tornado alley or near a nuclear reactor. You need to have a second location just in case your home is destroyed or it isn't safe to be in. This is also helpful for your family members just in case you are separated or are not together when it is time to bug out. Make sure you designate a route for each family member to follow as well as a backup route in case the first is compromised. If a bridge is out or the traffic is too bad, you need to have a second option. Think back to the map on the back of the hotel door. You need a clear route. The shortest route is always better, but it may not always be an option.

Choose a second location that is relatively out of sight. If you can invest in fencing and other security measures, it would be a good idea. Set up a solar panel or two as an alternative energy means. Start collection rainwater. Do what you can today to make that location as safe and as comfortable as possible. Visit the location from time to time with your family to make sure they are familiar with it. Practice getting there during different seasons, different times of the day, and in different scenarios. When disaster strikes, it can be extremely difficult to deal with emotionally. Having a familiar place to hole up in will provide comfort at a time when it is sorely needed. If you have children, make sure you have a few of the toys they like and any special blankets or other comfort measures available. If you have pets, don't forget to stock some kibble or any other supplies, if you plan on taking them with you.

The second location is one that you will want to keep fairly under wraps. You don't want to advertise the fact to neighbors, co-workers and others who are not a part of your prepping plan. People will get desperate in the aftermath of a disaster if they have not done their own prepping. They will be willing to do things they wouldn't normally do to stay alive. Keep the second location known only to those who you trust the most, and only those who you wouldn't mind trying to survive with, if it comes to that!

5) Create or Update Your Emergency Contact List (and make sure everyone in your family knows it!)

You will want to create an emergency contact list. Most of us rely on our cell phones to store all of our contacts. Many of us don't even know our parent's or kids' phone numbers by memory. We simply find their name in our phone books and push a button. If your cell phone is broke or the battery is dead, you won't have any way to access those numbers. What if the grid is down – how will you contact anyone?

Take the time today to create a list of important names, numbers, and addresses. Print copies to keep in your emergency binder and give one to each member of the family. It is a good idea to write the numbers and addresses on a notecard and seal the card with clear contact paper to protect it from moisture. For little kids, write the information on a piece of fabric and either sew it into their backpack or inside their jacket. If disaster strikes when you are away from your child, you want them to be able to contact you or call for help.

There are some key people that you will want to have contact information for, above all others. Of course, the people you contact and the order in which you call them will depend on what type of disaster you are dealing with. Some examples include:

- Sheriff/state police numbers besides 911
- Family member who lives in another area to check in with
- Each family member's individual number
- School numbers for each child
- Daycare phone number
- Work phone numbers
- Local hospital number
- Red Cross

You have to assume emergency services are going to be taxed following a disaster. Calling 911 may not work. You need to be able to call the police directly. If something happens and you need to pick up your kids at a different time or you need to have somebody else pick up the child, you will want to have the school number. The Red Cross will likely be called in within a few days. They will have a number for family members to call and register with so you can all get in touch just in case you lose contact with your loved ones. Addresses are equally important to have. In the even the phone grid goes down, you need to have a way to reach your family or other important contacts. Having phone numbers will not be enough in these situations, so make sure you have addresses as well, at least for a few vital people or places. As we said before, have a backup for your backup – you never know which one you'll need!

6) Figure Out Who Will Be a Part of Your Overall Survival Plan (family, friends, neighbors)

Many preppers are very secretive about their prepping. They hide it, lie about it and do their best to make excuses as to why there are 15 gallons of water stashed under the sink. Sometimes that can be a good strategy. Then again, sometimes that can backfire. It is best if you include at least a few people that you can trust in your planning. You can't do it all alone, no matter how much you believe in yourself. You don't want to me a lone survivor. It would be extremely difficult to take care of everything needed for survival on your own. There are simply too many factors to consider. Too many variables. Too many small, tiny things that could go wrong if you're all by yourself. There is also the fact it would be pretty lonely. Who knows how long a disaster scenario will last – do you really want to be all by yourself for what could turn out to be a very, very long time indeed?

Your immediate family, spouse, kids and anybody else who lives in the home should all be included in the planning process, at the very minimum. You need to talk with them about what you are doing, why you are doing it, and how they should all be able to get involved. Talk them through each step of the plan so they can be involved and prepared to jump right in without you having to take the time to explain the what and why. There is always a possibility you will not be home to act as the coordinator when disaster strikes. They need to know what to do to get your plans in motion, and where and how they will meet up with you later. You also have to consider the possibility of you being injured and unable to activate the plan of action. If you're not around, surely you still want your family to survive, right?!

If you have friends or neighbors that you trust, you can include them in your plan. Sometimes your skills can benefit each other in ways that you wouldn't have even thought of. Imagine if you are an expert gardener and your neighbor is quite the handyman. You are setting yourself up for success when you put together a team of individuals with different areas of expertise. You will be able to complement each other, which will aid in your survival. Divide and conquer is a very effective way to tackle all the little jobs that will need to be handled after a disaster.

It is also helpful to include others in the early stages of your planning process so you can bounce ideas off of each other. Sometimes your initial plan may have holes in it that you wouldn't be able to identify without a different perspective. Having another set of eyes to look over your plans, share their plans, and expose you to new ideas, can really be beneficial for your overall prepping strategy. Choose who you will involve in your prepping process wisely. Make sure they are people you can trust, as much as possible. Even still, don't give all of your plans away to anyone except your family and closest confidants. It would be wise to keep some pertinent details, like your second location or hidden stash of money, to yourself. Unfortunately, you can't always trust everybody; your family would be the exception.

Assign tasks for each person involved in your prepping. If you are involving neighbors or friends and family, consider planning monthly or weekly meetings to talk about what you have done and what needs to be done. This is a great way to pool resources and take some of the financial burden off of yourself. It also keeps you focused on short-term goals that will help you achieve your long-term survival needs. You will have the benefit of using ideas from your fellow preppers. People can get pretty resourceful and there are often little tips or tricks that you wouldn't have thought of yourself. You want every advantage possible and if that means borrowing ideas from your fellow prepper, so be it. We all have the same goal and we all can learn a lot from each other.

7) Start Stockpiling Basic Food and Water (Start Early, Stock Often)

This is the part you have been waiting for! Or, at least, the part you knew was fairly obvious. You can't be a prepper unless you actually prep food and water, right? Right you are! You need to start thinking about what it is you want to store in case of an emergency, and what you really, definitely, absolutely *need* to store. Don't buy a bunch of canned spinach and beets that your family doesn't like just because they are super cheap. One of the most important rules of preparing a food storage is to only store what you would eat today. Your taste buds are not going to change just because there is an emergency. You are not suddenly going to decide anchovies are your favorite food. Don't waste your money on food that will leave your family longing for the good ol' days, *when* there are equally good choices. Sure, if you're all starving and haven't eaten in days following a disaster, you'll eat beets or anchovies in a heartbeat! But, if you could have spent $0.10 extra and gotten canned tuna instead, which you all love, doesn't it make sense to go for that option now?! Yes, of course it does.

You will need to come up with a plan of action to build up your food storage. What is your goal? How far in advance do you have the capabilities to prep for? How much space is in your prepping pantry? A good way to start is by planning a 3-month food storage, as a minimum. This helps you build up to the 1-year supply that many preppers aim for. You will want to do some basic math when it comes to planning how much food you need, depending on how many members of your family and your ages. You can go about this in couple of different ways.

The first would be to focus solely on calories. Technically, in survival mode, you are not eating for joy; you are eating to stay alive and healthy. You only need a certain amount of calories per day to do this. Plan on each family member eating 2000 calories per day (though they could easily get by on less, depending on age, size, gender, etc). Take a look at some of the food labels on the items your family likes or regularly eats. How much would a person need to eat to reach their daily calorie requirement? Are there better choices (cheaper, healthier) that could reach those goals more easily? Are there other options that have a longer shelf life and would be a much better fit for a prepping pantry? These are the types of questions to ask as you narrow down the types of foods you want to start buying and storing.

The second option would be to examine how much food you typically serve your family at each meal. Do you use one, two or three cans of soup to satisfy the family at lunch? Multiply that number by let's say 12, assuming you would serve that meal once a week for 12 weeks. How much rice do you usually go through in, say, a month? Focus on the most shelf-stable items and the ones that are most easily storable. You want to build the foundation of your pantry based off of these types of items. Many people make the mistake of not looking far enough ahead. For example, you say your family loves sandwiches and eats them every single day for lunch? So you want to store a couple loaves of bread? Forget it! Do you know how quickly bread goes bad? It's not even worth storing one loaf (unless you plan on eating it before the week is out!) So don't always focus on the things your family loves and eats the most; focus on the things with the longest shelf life!

Along the same lines - don't make the dangerous mistake of storing 100 cans of refried beans or chicken noodle soup and assume your family can live on the same meal every single day for a few months. There is a very real thing called food fatigue that can develop from eating the same food, day in and day out. Food fatigue causes intestinal upset and could ultimately lead to dehydration. That is not something you want to be dealing with when water is going to be in short supply. Buy with some variety and plan on serving different foods as frequently as it is viable to do so. Your taste buds, and your tummy, will thank you.

That brings us to our next topic—water storage. Everyone knows that we need water to survive, but how much is actually enough? It's safe to say you need, at the bare minimum, one gallon of water per day for each member of the family. If you plan on keeping your pets with you, you need to factor in their water needs as well. If you can't store enough water for your family, you need to store a water purification method to clean the water you gather. ALL water you collect is considered dangerous to drink without purifying first. So, how to go about collection and storing all of that water?

You have plenty of options to storing water. As part of your planning process, investigate some of the various ways you can gather or simply store water, like rain barrels and stackable water walls, which are 3-gallon square jugs that fit together to form a solid wall. This can be a huge space saver and gives you the luxury of being able to take an empty container off the wall so you can refill it whenever it is needed.

Take a walk around your neighborhood or the location you will be hunkering down in to find the nearest water sources. Ideally, you should look for water that is within a few miles of your abode. You don't want to be hauling water several miles each way on a daily basis. It could be dangerous and it will tax your energy. Look for streams or river, or sources of fresh water. If the only options are lakes or salt water, you are definitely going to need to have a large stock of water purification tablets in your storage pantry. These can be found in camping or outdoor sports stores, as well as in many places online. They typically have a fairly long shelf life, so feel safe loading up on as many as you think you will need. And then, when you have that number calculated, add on a few more, for extra measure! You can never be too safe when it comes to planning your water supplies – if you fail on that prep, nothing else will matter.

8) Prep Your Body and Mind!

Speaking of walking to collect water and then carrying back a 5-gallon jug of water - could you even do it? In your current state, would you get tired? Are you in decent physical condition? One of the major parts of prepping that many tend to overlook is the sheer physical nature of surviving. Lets face it: right now, we have it pretty easy. We turn on the tap when want water, we turn on the heater when we are cold, and when we are hungry, we open the freezer and pop something into the microwave. In a post-traumatic event world, ALL of those luxuries will be gone. If you want water, you have to find it and clean it. If you are cold, you have to find and chop the wood to build a fire. If you are hungry, you have to actually prepare a meal and either eat it cold or build a fire to cook it. It will take a lot longer than what you are accustomed to, and it will require a whole heck of a lot more energy than we ever use on those same tasks right now. It only makes sense, then, that now is the perfect time to get your body and mind in order, so that you'll be able to do all those necessary tasks to survive.

You need to get yourself and your whole family in good physical condition so you all are better able to handle the physical demands of life without electricity, running water or transportation. If you are overweight and are not currently active, you need to change it, now. Can you physically walk 10 miles or swing an axe in your current physical shape? If you can't, you need to start walking a little every day. Start building up your stamina so you are ready. Start small, but start today. Get the whole family involved. If you have little ones, you may have to carry them if you have to bug out to another location. Consider getting a wagon or cart that you can pull the little ones in.

If you have knee problems or other issues that will give you trouble in a physical world, keep a knee brace, back brace or whatever on hand to help aid you. Some of us are not quite as youthful as we once were, but there are ways to accommodate those little hiccups.

Part of your conditioning should include tasks that you would likely need to do in a survival situation. Things like chopping wood, carrying water, gardening, building a fire and walking long distances over hills are all likely activities when you are living in a world turned upside down. If I had to guess, I bet you currently don't do many, if any, of these vital activities. You can't just expect to magically jump into action, physically and mentally, when you haven't practiced any of those important tasks, can you? Of course not! You plan your prepping so thoroughly that you owe it to yourself to make sure you're in physical shape to be able to carry out your plans. Prepare yourself today so you are not struggling at a time when you simply cannot afford to be down and out.

9) Begin Getting Your Money and Finances in Shape (Prep Your Budget!)

There are plenty of scenarios that could thrust the world into something from the Dark Ages. Not every scenario will necessarily result in a collapse of the financial system. That means those bills you have today are still going to be there when things *do* get crazy. The last thing you want to deal with is a bill collector hunting you down and demanding payment. Can you survive both physically and financially?

You need to do your best to get your finances in shape now. Eliminate as much debt as you can. Make a concerted effort to manage your finances better. Live within your means. Don't go into debt in order to prep. If you currently live paycheck to paycheck, take a hard look at your existing expenses and find ways to cut costs.

Prepping, like buying food, water and other supplies, will take money to do. You don't want to max out your credit cards trying to stock up on things. The best way to create a healthy food storage that will sustain your family is to do it a little at a time in a way you can afford. Buy a few extra cans of food each time you go grocery shopping and add them to your food storage. Cut coupons. Buy things on sale. Adopt thrifty shopping habits and you will be so much better off.

Putting the family on a budget that frees up some of your current monthly income to put towards prepping is crucial. Often times, we say "Oh, we can buy that next week or next month when we don't have this bill or that bill." Guess what? There are always going to be those little bills that pop up. You'll never start prepping if you use this mindset. You have to change your lifestyle a bit to get out of debt and stay out while contributing to your emergency storage plan.

If you have extra "stuff" lying around the house just taking up space, consider having a yard sale to get rid of the stuff while making some extra cash. Use the cash to pay off a debt or to put towards buying food for your emergency storage. Tighten up your expenditures by cooking meals at home and making every dollar stretch. If you don't have to buy new—don't. Buy used and save some money. Work to get every last bit of use out of your tools, clothing, shoes and so on. Make leftovers a weekly meal instead of throwing them out.

Many preppers are investing in gold and silver coins to use as currency in a world that has suffered an economic collapse. This is a good idea. To afford those gold and silver coins, you are going to have to find room in your budget to do so. Don't be afraid to offer to trade things you have for gold and silver. Bartering is going to be the way of the future so it doesn't hurt to start learning the ropes today.

10) The Family that Preps Together, Survives Together!

You may discover certain family members are not on board with your desire to being prepping. They make be skeptical or they may just not understand your mindset in the least. You may be ridiculed and called names and teased about the sky falling and so on. So be it. You are trying to do something that will save your family's life. It may take some effort to convince some members of the family, but you have to try. People outside your immediate family will likely have an opinion about your "crazy ideas," but let it roll off your shoulders. When things do go sideways, they will be knocking on your door begging for help. You'll be the one prepared.

If somebody is adamant they don't want to be involved in learning various ways to start a fire or how to purify water, that's fine. Try getting them involved in preparing a food storage that will keep the family fed for a few months. Ask them what they're interested in and tailor their involvement towards those ends. You don't have to tell them you are prepping for nuclear fallout or some other disaster that may scare them. Tell them you are preparing for the possibility you may be without work or somebody may get very ill and the hospital bills will make it difficult to put food on the table.

Some members may be hesitant to buy into prepping simply because they don't want to think about such frightening scenarios that could leave the world as they know it in upheaval. Try to remove the fear by focusing on the food or prep items themselves and not the whys. Ask each member of the family what their favorite food is or what kind of food would they want to eat if they couldn't leave the house for a week. Make it into a game or a fun thought exercise. They'll be much more likely to participate if you don't make it all about the doom and gloom situations.

Bring up some real-life scenarios that have happened, like Hurricane Katrina, Hurricane Sandy or the earthquake in Haiti. Point out that those people were forced to go without for several days. Plenty of people died while waiting for emergency services. They suffered through an already horrible situation. If the people had planned ahead and had enough food and water, their suffering wouldn't have been nearly as bad. Natural disaster can strike anywhere at any time. Try to get your family to realize that you want them to be safe and comfortable in case something does happen. It isn't crazy!

Start out small and slowly work them into prepping. Picking food they want on the shelves and helping you organize is one way to work them into prepping. Make it an adventure when you talk about the different routes you would take in case you had to leave your home to a second location. Make your practice runs more about spending time together as a family rather than preparing for disaster. They will be learning the route without getting hung up on why they are learning it.

Lastly, don't push. If you have somebody that is truly reluctant, don't force the issue. Make sure they know where to go and what to do in case of emergency, but don't expect them to do much in the way of helping you prepare. Everybody comes to the understanding that prepping is a lifesaving tool in their own time. Don't let it discourage you.

Conclusion

So there you have it. 10 concrete things that you can get started on today to make sure you and your loved ones are heading down the right path. They aren't huge, grand ideas. They are small, simple steps that you can easily start on today. They don't require a ton of money, or a ton of time. They just require you to be focused, dedicated, and to really want to take the first steps towards securing your future.

Prepping often gets a bad rap these days. People have a lot of pre-conceived ideas of it. Most of them are wrong. Prepping isn't crazy. Prepping isn't the most difficult thing a family can do. It doesn't have to be complicated. It doesn't have to be expensive. It can even be fun! The most important thing is that you simply start. Start now. There's no better time! As they say, the earlier you start, the better off you'll be when you really need it.

Good luck, fellow Preppers!

*****

Bug Out Bag Basics

Introduction

Life can change in the blink of an eye. We all know that, whether we're preppers or not. Some think the world as we know it will end due to pandemics, food shortages, power grid failures, or nuclear disasters, but something far less dramatic could make it necessary to leave your home and head to a secure location. A coming hurricane, a wildfire, or even a prolonged power outage can leave you stranded and helpless if you're not prepared. If you don't have somewhere else to go or, at the very least, a Bug Out Bag (BOB) and a plan, what will you do?

Thanks to television and the Internet, preppers have become known for stockpiling supplies in preparation for such events. Some have built bunkers in their homes or on their property, with food and water supplies that can last years. In a crisis situation, though, a home stockpile could be quickly compromised as desperate looters come searching for food and medicine. Worse yet, what if your home is destroyed? What will you do then?

Since the goal here is to survive, and not die defending your canned beans, you've hopefully chosen a secure place to run to if things get too bad at home. This secure place is known as your bug out location, and to get there, you'll need a bug out bag.

What's that, you ask? Very simply, a bug out bag is a backpack or other easily portable container packed with enough essentials to get you safely from Point A to Point B. It's not a place to store every survival item you ever think you'll need. It's also not something extremely simple that you just carry a bottle of water and a couple of protein bars in. You can buy pre-assembled bug out bags online, but you don't need to spend a fortune to gather all the supplies you'll need. You can spend as much or as little as you want, as long as you have the essentials.

It's common to keep 72 hours worth of supplies in your bug out bag. That should be enough time for you and your family to either make it to your Plan B location, or to find somewhere else that has suitable shelter for you to set up base and regroup. After that, you'll need to find sustainable sources of food, water, and shelter. This book will examine the different categories of items that you'll want to stock up on for your bug out bag, as well as give you tips and tricks for making the most of your space. Hopefully, by the end of it, you'll be ready to start working on a bug out bag for you and your loved ones. In many possible situations, a bug out bag may very well be the difference between survival and not making it, so you want to do everything you can to prepare.

So, fellow Prepper, let's get to it!

Water

When it comes to survival, water is the most important supply you can have. This seems obvious, but oftentimes people take having easy access to drinkable water for granted. It's just something we're used to, so we think it will always be there. That can be prepping mistake #1. Take nothing for granted. You will need to plan, prep, or work for everything. Humans can survive a long time without food if necessary, but a lack of water, even for a few days, can be deadly.

Unfortunately, water is also one of the heavier, bulkier items you'll need in your bug out bag. To stay hydrated throughout a 72-hour bug out, you'll need approximately 256 ounces of water. That's more than 16 pounds, not including the bulky packaging that most commercially available water comes in. For some people, that's simply not feasible. So how do you make room for this essential commodity in your bug out bag?

If you have a means of transportation to take you to your bug out spot, like a car, boat, horse, or other motorized vehicle, the weight of the water won't be a problem. You can even store some water in your vehicle, to free up space in your bug out bag. But, you cannot rely on that option completely. When disaster strikes, your mode of transportation could fail, get stolen, or be destroyed, so you'll need a worst-case plan for lugging at least some, and maybe all, of that water around.

One option is to just pack containers of water in your bag. You'll obviously need a large backpack or rucksack for this, because 256 ounces of water is equivalent to 16 plastic bottles, or two 1-

gallon jugs. Not always possible, for some people. Of course, you could just strap or tape bottles of water to the outside of your pack, but the goal here is to carry just enough water to keep you alive until you can find a more permanent water source.

Some preppers only bring a liter of drinking water per day for their bug outs. They drink sparingly until they can find a more permanent source of water. This approach requires you to have a portable filtration system to make sure the water you find is safe to drink. You can use sport water bottles that come with filters, iodine tablets (read the directions carefully), or, the most portable option of all, the LifeStraw.

The LifeStraw is used by millions of people worldwide to filter natural water sources. You just stick one end into a lake, stream, or puddle, and suck up filtered water that is 99.9% free of waterborne bacteria, protozoa, and viruses. And at just 9" long and 2oz in weight, the LifeStraw is a wonderful addition to any survival pack. If you can spare the money, it's one of the better prepping investments you can make, and one that most people don't even know about.

Whatever method you choose – LifeStraw, purification tablets, homemade filter, or trying to carry as much bottled water as you can, this should be the first thing you address when building your bug out bag. The rest of your bag, and your survival plan, won't matter at all, if you don't have any drinkable water. Plan for a few different methods and spend some time testing them out. Practice using a LifeStraw or purification tablets, or practice trying to carry around full 2-liter bottles in a backpack. You need to find the method that will work best for you and your family, and you need to be well-versed on how you are going to execute that plan. Practice makes perfect!

Food

After water, the next most obvious item you will want to pack into your bug out bag is food. We can survive longer without food than we can without water, but we still need food to function, especially in a survival situation.

FEMA and the Red Cross advise everyone to have storage of or access to at least 3 days worth of food in the event of an emergency. This is a good benchmark to have for your bug out bag as well. Since you're going to burn a lot of calories carrying your bug out bag to your destination, you need to pack food items that are small, lightweight, non-perishable, nutrient-dense, and high in calories. It's easy to find prepackaged prepper meals online, but be careful with the nutrition content of some of these - you need to make sure that your food has a good blend of carbohydrates, for fast energy, and fat and protein, for sustained energy.

Meals, Ready-to-Eat (known as MREs) are a popular choice for portable food. They are used in the military by soldiers in the field and provide approximately 1,200 calories per meal, with a good carb to fat ratio. Three of these meals will meet your daily caloric needs, as well as your vitamin and mineral requirements. They're fairly easy to carry, since they are made for soldiers to carry around with them.

Military MREs (or their civilian counterparts) typically contain an entree, a side dish, a dessert, a drink mix, bread or crackers with a spreadable topping (usually peanut butter or cheese), seasonings, and plastic utensils. There are currently 24 varieties of military MREs to choose from, designated as menus 1-12 and menus 13-24. All of them come with a flameless heating element so that you can eat your meals warm.

The downside of filling your bag with MREs is the price: you could pay $40 - $60 for a case of 12 online, or as much as $80 per case at an Army surplus store. At these prices, it can be difficult to stock up for the entire family. The military does not directly sell MREs to civilians, but there are many companies that offer their own versions of MREs. You might get more variety with the commercial MREs, but their pricing is similar to the military ones, if not a bit more expensive.

If MREs aren't your thing, you can still find food that packs plenty of calories into a small serving size. You want your daily intake to consist of at least 2,500 calories (much more if you're carrying a heavy pack through difficult terrain) with a ratio of about 40% carbs, 30% fat, and 30% protein.

Peanut butter is a great choice, since a mere 2 Tbsp. serving contains 200 calories, 16g of fat, 6g of carbs, and 6g of protein. This is a great staple for any bug out situation. Just add some crackers, and you've got a nourishing snack to keep you fueled.

You can also make your own trail mix to snack on. Just take your choice of nuts and dried fruits (raisins are a popular choice), add in some cereal or M&Ms for more carbs and calories, and double-pack them in Ziploc baggies to keep air and moisture out.

For protein, packages of chicken and tuna are more lightweight than cans, and you can find them at pretty much any grocery store.

The single-serve pouches come in several different flavors, and though they are light in calories, they pack at least 14 grams of protein per pouch. Tuna is also a good source of B12, which is thought to support your body's metabolism and help you feel more energetic – always a plus in survival situations. Don't forget about beef or turkey jerky. These are easy to carry and pack quite a protein and nutrient punch. They can be a bit more expensive than traditional trail mix, but it's good to mix in a couple sticks of jerky for when you need a little extra protein and iron kick.

Protein bars are an excellent source of calories, vitamins and nutrients, and they come pre-packed in waterproof materials. Look for bars with high carbs and protein. Stay away from bars that are high in sugar or that are overly processed. These ones will fill you up with non-nutritious junk and could actually harm you, rather than provide the fuel you need to keep going.

Remember, the more (healthy) calories, the better. The goal is to get through your bug out so that you can survive another another day!

First Aid

A good first-aid kit can mean the difference between life and death in a disaster situation. Yet, a lot of people still seem to think that there is no way they will get injured enough to need a first aid kit and, thus, they don't bother packing one. Big mistake!

Hiking for miles through weeds and woodlands is bound to result in some uncomfortable scrapes or insect bites, but you should be prepared to deal with greater injuries such as sprains, trauma, bleeding, and life-threatening allergic reactions, until you have access to medical professionals. If you're bugging out with family members, the chances of at least one of you getting injured greatly increases and you will definitely want a first aid kit in one of your bug out bags.

Sprains and strains are fairly common, and while they aren't lethal, they can cause a lot of pain and really slow you down. You'll want to make sure your bug out first aid kit contains pressure bandages and cold packs, as well as some over-the-counter anti-inflammatory medicine, like Advil or Aleve, to reduce pain and swelling.

It never hurts to bring some Benadryl in cream or pill form in case you have a mild allergy attack. For more serious allergic reactions, an Epi-pen is recommended. Epi-pens are auto-injecting pens that deliver a dose of epinephrine, a powerful anti-allergy drug that can save lives. They can be quite expensive, but you can find coupons and discount cards online. Also, if your physician prescribes an Epi-pen, it should be covered by your insurance plan.

Just make sure you know how to use it before it is needed; practice pens and instructions can be found online.

Burns and blisters are another injury you might have to deal with. Unfortunately, there's not much you can do to treat burns in the field. Just make sure you have a quality burn-relief ointment in your first aid kit, along with cold packs and clean cloths that can be soaked in cool water. Dry, sterile gauze or cotton bandages can be used to dress the burn after you apply the cream. Bring enough to change the dressing twice a day.

Trauma and bleeding are two of the most dangerous injuries you can have, especially if you can't get to a hospital right away. Whether the trauma is from an accidental cut or fall, or a knife or bullet wound, your most immediate goal will be to stop the bleeding.

For smaller wounds, look for blood-clotting agents like Z-Medica's QuikClot sponges. They come in 25-gram and 50-gram pouches, and you can choose an anti-microbial version to help prevent infection. Blood-clotting agents can be found in outdoor and sporting goods stores.

Larger wounds might require stitches to stop the bleeding. It sounds intimidating because few people outside of the medical profession know how to stitch a wound properly. Luckily, we live in the Information Age! Get a quality suture kit for your first aid bag, and look up instructional videos to learn good suturing technique.

Tourniquets are another good supply to have in your bug out bag. They can be tightened around an arm or leg to prevent blood from flowing to that limb. However, many people consider tourniquets to be a last resort, since limbs can actually be lost because of them. But if none of the other methods have stopped the bleeding, a tourniquet can be a literal lifesaver.

Of course, tourniquets aren't useful for wounds to the torso. A gut wound can leave you bleeding out, and it's possible for a knife or bullet to puncture a lung, which is an incredibly serious injury that needs emergency care. For deep, penetrating injuries, you will need trauma pads and chest seals. Trauma pads absorb blood and can be used like a pressure dressing. Chest seals are heavy-duty gel pads that are placed directly over the wound. They conform to the body and seal the wound to stop serious bleeding. Both the trauma pads and the chest seals come in packages that weigh less than 2oz. That's a lot of lifesaving power that easily fits into a bug out bag.

If you're in an area that has a lot of smoke, dust, or ash in the air, you'll want to keep some face masks on hand. The basic tie-on masks won't protect you against viruses, but they can help filter the air you breathe in. Safety glasses will protect your eyes in similar situations.

Don't overlook the basics when you plan your first aid kit. You'll want some medical supplies to sterilize wounds and keep annoying personal problems at bay. Keep sterilized alcohol and iodine pads in your first aid kit, along with a hand sanitizer, and an antibiotic cream like Neosporin. Band-Aids and moleskin can cover simple wounds and blisters. You'll also want an anti-diarrheal drug like Imodium, because it's bad enough to be in a survival situation in the first place; you don't want to have the runs while you're on the run. If you take special medication, make sure that you pack enough to last 72 hours. You might want to consult with your doctor to see if you can take half-doses in emergency situations. (NEVER change your dosage without your doctor's approval!)

Finally, the first aid bag itself needs to be of good quality to protect its contents. Shop around until you find a good-sized bag that is sturdy and waterproof. If the kit won't fit inside your bug out bag, you can easily clip it to the outside. Learn and practice all of the above techniques, so that you are comfortable with applying first-aid in a real-life situation. You don't want the first time you try to bandage someone up to be when you're out on the road, fleeing from something, and trying to survive. You want to be comfortable and knowledgeable about what you're doing, so the time to start practicing is now. Make sure you're not the only one in the family or group who knows how to use the first-aid kit; someone might need to use it on you. Have everyone practice various safety and first-aid tasks. Make it a part of your survival preparations and you'll be that much better off, should you ever *really* need to use it.

Light

Another thing that people don't often think about or gloss over is the importance of light. Think about it for a minute. If you're out in the open, or on the run, what are you doing to after the sun goes down? Do you know how to survive in complete darkness? Can you find everything you need in your bag at night? Do you know how to seek shelter or pitch a tent in the dark? Light sources are extremely important for traveling and setting up camp at night. They will make survival easier and help family members feel much safer. One source isn't enough, usually. Make sure to have backups in case your main light source fails. You don't want to be relying on one light only, because if that fails, for any reason at all, you'll be completely in the dark.

LED lanterns are a good choice for primary light sources. Look for a small, weatherproof model like the Coleman 4AA Packaway, which weighs only 8oz. It also has a bright setting, an energy-saving setting, and an emergency strobe. This is a great, lightweight, all-in-one type of light that is easy enough for multiple family members to carry. Get one early and get familiar and comfortable with all of the settings and the different modes and methods of using it. It can be a real lifesaver out in the wild open at night.

Every bug out bag should also contain a small, dependable flashlight, or at least a keychain light, in case you just need a little bit of illumination and don't want to telegraph your location with a brighter light. These can be found for relatively little money, though many of them depend on a steady supply of batteries, so don't forget to pack an extra set at least. You don't want to be left without a light source simply because you didn't have an extra set of batteries. LED headlamps are also a choice and can light your path while leaving your hands free. While not suitable for every situation, they can be a good choice for certain individuals or families.

The military issues glowsticks to its soldiers in the field, and these little sticks have a variety of uses. They can also be a great choice for your bug out bag. You can use them to mark a trail, gauge the depth of a hole or crevice, or send messages using different colored sticks. They can also shed a bit of light if your other light sources don't work. They aren't the first choice for a source of light, but if you have extra room, and you have an idea of how to use them properly, they can be a really great addition to an experienced bug out bag.

Again, you'll want to make sure you have plenty of batteries to keep your lights shining. Don't cheap out on the batteries; stick with brands that are known to be dependable and long-lasting. There's nothing worse than planning and prepping and having it all be for nothing…because you forgot the batteries!

Clothing

This is a category that many people don't consider. They spend time and money stocking up a great bug out bag…and then they forget to think about what they will be wearing. Clothing should not be an afterthought. The clothing you bug out in will depend on your local climate, but you definitely want to be prepared if you encounter cold, wet conditions on your trek, or if you live somewhere with freezing winters or blazing summers. If you are not properly prepared in your clothing, nothing else in your bug out bag will matter.

Start with some basic items that are loose, light, and non-restrictive. Choose a long-sleeved shirt, some long pants, and a lightweight jacket or hoodie to begin. Some preppers believe in having all of their clothing be camouflage, all the time, but you can make yourself a target if you look like the prepper stereotype. Camo is good when you're in the woods, but it's best to use drab, neutral colors in most other setting. Choose garments that have plenty of pockets, and avoid any bright colors that will draw attention to you. Bring a cap or sunglasses to look a little more incognito and protect your eyes from bright light.

For cold weather, you'll need a parka or heavy winter coat, some thick gloves, and 2 – 3 pairs of thick socks. Bring a knit cap, safety goggles, and wool glove liners for extremely cold temperatures.

To stay dry in wet conditions, pack a heavy-duty poncho and wear waterproof hiking shoes or boots. If you find yourself sloshing around in cold water, you'll be glad to have them.

Packing the right clothing is one area where you can really get your family involved. If you have children, this is a great way to introduce them to the idea of prepping and to get them excited about the process. Ask them to help choose which clothing items they will bring. Maybe they have a favorite jacket or a favorite pair of socks. Explain why you are choosing the items that you are, based on the weather, your location, or things such as that. This will help them feel involved in the process and that excitement can make all of the difference later on down the road.

Some people will pack their bug out bag completely and then leave two sets of clothing off to the side: one for cold weather and one for warmer weather. This way, depending on the season it is when a survival event happens and you need to bug out, you can quickly grab the appropriate clothing for the season, grab your bug out bag, and get going. This also saves some space, as you don't need to pack extra clothes that you won't use. If you live somewhere that climate isn't as much of an issue, such as Southern California or Florida, you can feel safer packing your clothing inside the bug out bag, so you can simply pick up the bag and go, when the time comes. Whichever way you choose, don't forget this important category! You don't want to be stuck outdoors without the proper clothing, so start thinking of this category now, as you are building your bug out bag.

Shelter

Shelter is a basic human need, of course, and even more so in an emergency bug out situation. You don't know how long you'll be hiking or be on the road for before you reach a safe place to stay, so you'll want to bring your own portable shelter to shield yourself from the wind and cold. Remember, your bug out bag should be filled with emergency supplies to help you rough it until you can either build or find a more permanent shelter, so you're not going to be worried about carrying an entire tent with you or anything. Rather, you need to start thinking about basic items that will help shelter you temporarily, until you can find something more permanent. Your shelter items or tools will, of course, vary greatly, depending on which area of the country you are in or what season it is. So you will need to think of your specific situation and plan tools or items that will fit in accordingly.

The most basic way to protect yourself from hypothermia is to wrap yourself in an emergency Mylar blanket and hunker down somewhere as far away from the direct wind as possible. These blankets are extremely lightweight and very affordable, and they trap your body heat so that it stays put and keeps you warm. You can even get two-person Mylar sleeping bags, and Mylar tube-tents for quick warmth. At the very minimum, you'll want one Mylar blanket for each member of your family or group.

If you have the unfortunate circumstance of bugging out when it's raining, you will definitely want something to keep the water off of you. A lightweight tarp can be used to shelter you from the rain.

You can tie it between two trees and use it like a lean-to. A waterproof bivouac cover for your sleeping bag can also increase your odds of having a dry night.

You can supplement your portable shelter by learning how to use tree limbs and other nearby items as support structures and camouflage. There are instructional videos online, as well as many books that can teach you this skill.

Finding shelter, or learning how to construct a quick place to spend one night, is one of those skills that you really need to practice and be comfortable with before a true survival event happens. This is one skill that you should take a weekend with your family and go out camping. Practice using just blankets, practice constructing a quick lean-to with a tarp and a couple of trees, and practicing finding shelter behind bigger rocks or other items to protect from the wind. If you have children that are younger, you can even start practicing just by spending a night in your backyard. This will help get them used to sleeping outdoors and you can practice building a simple tent on the grass. All of this time spent practicing will help you and your family develop the skills that will be necessary in a real survival event. So start early and practice often.

Personal Hygiene

The end of the world is no excuse for bad hygiene! Well, maybe you can let the eyebrow tweezing and aftershave slide for a while, but personal hygiene is more about keeping yourself healthy than about looking or smelling nice. If you've made the decision to bug out, it's a safe bet that something has gone horribly wrong. You don't want to have to contend with toothaches, skin infections, or ingrown toenails while you're trying to survive. The better hygiene you practice, the less likely it is that you will suffer from these easily-preventable issues.

First, you're going to have to decide which items you truly need, and which would just be adding weight to your bag with little reward. Look for items that can be used in multiple ways, like a Swiss Army Knife that includes nail clippers and scissors. Dr. Bronn's Magical Soaps come highly recommended, since they are all-natural and can be used as body wash, shampoo, dish soap, laundry soap, etc. These liquid soaps can be purchased online in 16 and 32 ounce bottles. One bottle of that should be enough to keep you clean, keep your supplies clean, and clean up anything else you will need in a bugging out scenario.

You can also pack some basic items in a waterproof Ziploc bag: a toothbrush, toothpaste, dental floss, cornstarch or baby powder, lip balm, sun screen, comb or brush, hair ties, and wet napkins for your hands. Use travel-sized items to save space and weight. These can easily be found at your local department store or bought online in bulk to save even more money.

Women and babies have special needs. Women will need sanitary napkins or tampons, and babies will need diapers. You can save space by going cloth instead of disposable for a few days. Diaper rash ointment is another good supply to keep on hand, since it can be used for a number of skin conditions for all ages. Remember – the bug out bag should only have enough supplies to last for 72 hours or so, so you don't need to go overboard stocking items that you won't use in that time. It's a fine line between being prepared and having too many things that simply weigh you down.

And now we come to the part of bugging out that nobody likes to imagine: the bathroom activities. You will almost certainly hear Nature's Call during these 72 hours, so you'll need some supplies to clean yourself with. Toilet paper is good, but bulky, so you might want to consider baby wipes as an alternative. They are moistened, so you will probably need only one to get sufficiently clean, and they come in thick packs that will last a good while. Just be sure that you have a way of storing them so that they don't dry out. If baby wipes won't work, you can carry packages of Kleenex. These come in little square packages that are small enough for each member of the family to carry a couple in their bag. Get extra-thick ones, as Kleenex tend to be a lot thinner than toilet paper. However, they will get the job done. Just make sure you also have a bottle of anti-bacterial gel in your bag for clean up afterwards.

This is one area that most Preppers don't like to think, or talk, about. But proper sanitation and keeping yourself clean can mean the difference between catching some bug or virus and staying healthy. When you're out in the elements in a survival situation, you need to do everything possible to stay clean and to stay healthy, so don't overlook this vital part of your bug out bag.

Communication

One of the most frightening aspects of bugging out is losing contact with friends, family, and news reports. You need to stay informed about what's going on in your area, and you will probably want to check in on your loved ones as well. We're a cellphone-crazy world, but what would happen if the cell towers failed, or became overloaded like they did after 9/11? What if your phone simply broke or got stolen? Luckily, there are still some old-school ways to keep communication alive in the Electronic Age.

Shortwave radios are good to have so that you can hear weather alerts and other emergency broadcasts. There are many styles to choose from, but you should look for one with a hand crank and solar panels so that you never have to worry about it running out of juice. The Safe-T-Proof emergency shortwave radio is a favorite, and it even comes with a flashlight and a cell phone charger, in case your phone is still a viable option.

Ham radios are a good way to stay in touch with others in your area. It's easy to get a ham radio operator's license, and most people have switched to amateur radio from the older CB radios. Ham radios are also available with many features, including some that are small and waterproof. If you go this route, do some research on how to operate the radio with a stealth antenna. It can't hurt to learn how to make a basic receiver or AM transmitter from scrounged items, either.

Finally, let's take it way back and not forget the usefulness of a good old pencil and paper. Keep these on hand, along with a waterproof permanent marker, in case you have to leave a note for someone on your front door, or in case you need to post a sign or warning on the trail. Practice communicating with your family or group using non-cellphone methods. Make it a game. This way, when the time comes, you'll all feel comfortable and confident that you'll be able to communicate vital information, no matter what.

Tools

It always helps to have the right tool for the right job, and bugging out is no exception. You might find yourself needing to dig a hole, repair tears in your gear, or whack your way through tall, dense underbrush. If you get caught without the right tools, your 72 hours will be a lot harder to survive than they need to be.

The first tool you need is a good, strong knife. In fact, you will probably want to have more than one. A non-folding knife with a carbon steel blade, preferably with a partly serrated edge, can be an excellent tool for sharpening sticks, shaving tinder, cutting cordage, and many other tasks. It can also be used as a hand-to-hand weapon in a combat situation. Look for one with a 5" blade or longer, and full-tang. That means the knife is one solid piece of metal from the tip of the blade to the end of the handle. Full-tang knives are very strong, and you don't have to worry about the blade breaking off at an unfortunate time.

A pocketknife is also very handy, like the Swiss Army Knife mentioned earlier, or a Leatherman multi-tool. You can find less expensive alternatives, but this is another item you don't want to low-ball. Choose a knife with many good reviews regarding its sturdiness. Don't fall for the "latest and greatest" craze. You don't need every new knife that comes out. Find a trusted, reliable brand that has been around for generations. This will last longer and do everything you could ever possibly need it for.

Many preppers are fans of e-tools, or entrenching tools. It's easy to see why: these sharp, serrated spades are excellent for digging and cutting. They are also lightweight, foldable for easy storage, and can be used in self-defense. They have been standard issue for US military personnel since 1870, and there is evidence that the Roman Legions used them thousands of years ago. Talk about standing the test of time!

Machetes are great tools for clearing a trail, and they can easily double as a weapon. Don't forget to bring something to keep your blades sharp, such as a high grain whetstone, or a hand-held sharpening tool that you can easily pass over the blade to give it a great edge. Look for favorably reviewed sharpeners on Amazon.

During the 72-hour bug out, you will likely find yourself in need for fire for warmth, wildlife deterrence, or cooking. Just like backup knives, you will want to have backup fire-building methods at your disposal. A flint-and-steel strike kit is all you really need to ignite dry tinder, but don't rely on it as your soul source of flame. Bring along a lighter and some waterproof, strike-anywhere matches. Some preppers like to bring a flame accelerant, like kerosene, but the safety of hauling around such a flammable liquid is debatable. Always exercise caution if you decide to add fuel to your fire.

Duct tape is one product that no bug out bag should be without. It can be used to bind limbs, patch holes in clothing, reinforce structures, and secure items to your pack, belt, or clothing. There's not much you can't accomplish with enough duct tape.

Rope is another must-have. A good 50-foot length of nylon paracord doesn't cost much, and it can be folded to take up minimal space in your bag. You can use its incredible tensile strength to suspend or secure items, or you can unravel a bit of the cord to use as thread.

While you're assembling all of these cool items into your pack, don't forget about the basic usefulness of a good sewing kit and a compass. You might need to make repairs while you're en route to your bug out location, and a needle and thread will keep you from having to get too creative. And while there are compass apps for every Smartphone, it's best to carry a magnetic compass to keep you moving in the right direction.

Remember: the best tools are only as good as the person using them. So start practicing with all of your tools. Make sure you know how to use them properly. Even the most fancy, most expensive tools are going to be completely worthless in a survival situation if you have no idea what to do with them. Practice often and practice in all types of situations. If you do that, you'll be comfortable surviving and getting the most out of your tools.

Extras

We've covered the essentials of a well-stocked bug out bag. Now let's take a look at some items that it would be nice to have, if you can spare the room and expense. Some readers might consider some of these items to be necessities; it all depends on how much you want to carry for 72 hours.

First, let's discuss firearms. Some people consider them a must-have, while others think that carrying a gun is asking for trouble. The choice to carry or not to carry depends on your personal convictions and the bug out situation you find yourself in. Preppers who do pack firearms suggest having a reliable pistol as well as a rifle. Always use firearms responsibly, and as a last resort to settle dangerous confrontations. If you're traveling with others, make sure that you and they know good firearm safety habits.

If you're carrying MREs in your bag, you will find that they contain drink mixes to add to your water. If you're packing your own food items instead of MREs, powdered drink mixes can help you consume enough water to stay healthy. Get some of the Powerade or another electrolyte drink that comes in single-serving packages that you can just dump into a bottle of water. If you need caffeine to get you through the day, you'll definitely need it to get through a bug out situation. Instant tea and coffee can provide quick energy, or you can splurge on a portable stove and complete mess kit so that you can brew your drinks the old fashioned way.

Mosquito netting is nice to have if you live in a climate where insects thrive. You can drape it around your tent to keep the critters out, and you can also purchase hats that come covered with mosquito netting. If netting is out of your price range, at least bring a good spray can of insect repellant to decrease your chances of getting a disease or an infected bite from those darned mosquitoes.

Face masks are important to avoid breathing polluted air, but the basic types won't protect you from airborne diseases. To get the best protection, you'll want to have an N95 particulate respirator and mask. Be sure to wear your safety glasses as well, to keep particles from entering your body through your eyes. N95 respirators are approved for stopping airborne bacteria and tuberculosis, among other particles.

Construction grade garbage bags are often overlooked, but they can make your trek much more comfortable. Some people stuff them with leaves and use them like a pad on which to place their sleeping bags. Others use them to catch drinkable condensation. In a pinch, they can also double as sleeping bag covers, waterproof blankets, and waterproof storage bags.

While a bug out is far from a vacation, you should consider bringing items that will make it more tolerable for everyone involved. Do you like card games? A single deck of playing cards can be used for many, many different games. If you prefer dominoes, bring a mini set of those in your bag. In fact, many popular games now come in travel-sized versions that are small and easy to pack. Games help keep your mind sharp, encourage interaction, and can ease the mind during stressful situations. They are also good for keeping kids occupied when they get bored or scared.

If you have a favorite candy or dessert, bring it along. Food is a great source of comfort for many, and the familiarity of a favorite taste will help keep your spirits up in otherwise troubling times. (Plus, you might need the extra calories.) Also consider bringing along some reading materials, if you're the reading sort. An inspirational or religious book can be very comforting. Even books you've read many times can bring comfort, and you can read them out loud to others.

Bugging out with children is a special challenge. You will want to make sure they have their favorite foods, a few toys, and something that soothes them, such as a pacifier for infants, or a special blanket or stuffed animal for older children. Crayons and coloring books are inexpensive, but they can provide hours of entertainment. Teens might enjoy reading a field guide that teaches them how to tell edible plants from harmful ones, and how to perform basic first aid measures.

Finally, it's a good idea to have items to barter, and a little cash. Cigarettes and alcohol are always in demand, as are sweets and ammunition. Most preppers recommend keeping about $20 in your bag, along with quarters in case you find a payphone that works.

Conclusion

Hopefully, this guide has shown you what you'll need to pack in a good quality bug out bag. You can't go wrong by following Maslow's Hierarchy of Needs: water, food, shelter, and safety must be your primary concerns. Everything else can wait until those needs are fulfilled.

Of course, the more items you put in your bug out bag, the more comfortable your 72 hours could be. Then again, if you pack too much, you'll put undue stress on your body and increase your caloric needs by carrying the extra weight. In the end, you must be the one to decide how much you need to bring. It's a fine balancing act between having too little and too much. Try to pack items that can be used in multiple ways, and look for lightweight versions of food containers and utensils. You need to pack for your specific situation, not for exactly what someone else tells you.

As the old saying goes, it's wise to expect the best, but prepare for the worst. Our culture is so dependent on electronics that hackers or system failures could bring our whole economy to a standstill. Extreme weather or solar flares could knock out our power for an unknown length of time. In an event like that, it would be every man for himself, as everyone struggled to survive the chaos. Remember that low-tech alternatives to our modern gadgets can be invaluable in an emergency.

Hopefully, none of us will ever need to grab our bug out bags and go, but it's better to be safe than sorry. Start packing today. Practice bugging out for a night or a weekend. Make sure your family or group is prepared with their bug out bags, and that they know how to use them. The more comfortable you are with your bug out bag, and the items inside, the better off you'll be when the time comes to actually use it. And that's what it's all about: Being prepared.

Good luck, fellow Preppers!

*****

Top 10 Prepping Mistakes (and How to Avoid Them!)

Prepping for a disaster is becoming quite trendy. Though it has always been practiced by a variety of people, over generations and generations, lately it has begun to take on a new importance. It is widely talked about and discussed freely in popular culture. There are plenty of people who are diving into prepping in an attempt to get ahead of the game, so to speak. There are also plenty of people who want to know what all the fuss is about.

Ten years ago, prepping was regarded as one of those things crazy people who lived deep in the forests did. Today, more and more people are seeing the sound reasoning behind prepping. We've seen natural disasters, governmental instability, wars and disease reaching our shores, and more. Even the government has advised every household to be prepared to live at last three days without assistance by storing food, water and other emergency gear. Clearly, there *is* something to this whole prepping thing, and more and more people are quickly catching on. With the increased interest in prepping, there are plenty of people who are a bit lost and just following the trend. They are jumping into prepping with both feet and grabbing this and that with no real purpose. It's not the most effective way!

Prepping is a little art, a little science and a lot of experience. New preppers are prone to making some big mistakes that could cost them and their families in the long run. In fact, it isn't just new preppers who are making mistakes. There are plenty of so-called veteran preppers who have gotten so focused on one thing, that they are leaving themselves vulnerable to other issues. The good news: the mistakes are fixable. However, you have to be able to identify the mistakes before you can correct them. Choosing who to listen to and follow is going to be your biggest hurdle. Ideally, you should do research and base your own decisions on the information you have gathered from various reputable sources. Don't accept anything at face value. If you are not certain about a particular statement, research it and get a second opinion. Prepping isn't all about following the latest trends and gurus, or trying to do what everybody else is doing. The best thing you can do as a prepper is to tailor and customize your prepping for YOU. Focus on you and your family and your specific needs. Everything else will fall into place.

The following pages include the top ten mistakes preppers, new and old, tend to make. They are culled from hundreds of interviews that I've done with people all over the nation over the past years. In talking with them, I see the same mistakes come up over and over again. Do yourself a favor and avoid falling into any one of these traps. Examine your current prepping habits through the lens of these common mistakes and decide which areas you need to change. You may just be saving your life and the lives of your family members by avoiding these practices. You *will* definitely save yourself a lot of frustration when the event you have been preparing for actually happens. Too often, we discover mistakes too late. And in the prepping game, that can mean the difference between surviving or not. But this is not new, completely unknown advice.

There are others out there who have found out these mistakes so that you don't have to. You don't need to reinvent the prepping wheel. Learn from other's mistakes!

#1 - Focusing On Just One Type of Prepper Event

This is a big one. One of the most common mistakes known in the prepping world. If you have ever checked out some blogs or watched *that* famous prepping show on television, you have probably noticed the person writing the blog or featured on the program was focused on one particular situation that could thrust the country into a world where it would truly be survival of the fittest and most prepared. One situation only. Their entire prep is geared towards only one possible event happening. See the mistake yet?

Focusing all of your energy on preparing for a pandemic will leave you vulnerable to an event like a total collapse of the dollar or the power grid. What if you're prepping for governmental collapse and then, whoops, along comes a huge natural disaster? While some preps are interchangeable, you will notice some people will spend a lot of their time, energy, and money investing in biohazard suits, plastic sheets and face masks to ride out a pandemic, but ignore things like backup power sources or avoid stocking up on items that can be used for bartering. What good is a biohazard suit going to do you if the collapse stems from the power grid going down?

There are plenty of events that could turn our world upside down. Natural disasters. Governmental collapse. Power grids going down. Wars. Medical emergencies. And on and on. So, it should go without saying, we have no way of predicting what will be the cause of the next big event where prepping will come into play. Keep your preps rather generic and you will be better off. Ensuring you are prepared for anything is the best way to go. Don't get too hung up on one specific potential event. Getting too specific in your prepping will leave you vulnerable to *all* of the other possible hazards that could come our way. These are some of the things that could leave you on your own and fighting to survive.

- Foreign or domestic war
- EMP (electro-magnetic pulse)
- Government collapse
- Power Grid failure
- Natural Disaster
- Diseases
- Dollar collapse

There is always the risk you will be faced with a combination of events. For example, as we've seen in the past few years, when there is a major natural disaster, it usually causes the power grid to fail. People who were not prepared will take to the streets to find or fight for what they need, creating a need for martial law. It's not speculation. We've seen it happen, over and over throughout the past 10 years. It only takes one disaster to set off a chain of events. You have to be ready to deal with anything and everything.

Obviously you cannot prep for every single possible event in the entire world. That's not what I'm suggesting. But you *can* and *should* prep items or prep in a way that will allow you to use your prep and your skills in a variety of events. Don't become too focused on one single, solitary event happening. You'll better your chances of survival if you prep for multiple events. Remember: look at the big picture!

#2 - Relying Only on Yourself (and Ignoring Like-Minded Others)

Another major misconception is that your prepping should be top-secret information, not to be shared with anybody except for your immediate family members. This is actually dangerous. Can you do everything *all* by yourself? Do you really want to be a lone survivor? Or, do you want to try and fight off a gang of bandits by yourself? What happens if you get injured? Who will take over until you're back to full-strength. Or, God forbid, what happens if you're no longer around? Who will take care of your family? Or will they know how to survive because you've taught them well? Keeping your prepping a secret helps nobody and potentially does a great deal of harm to you and your loved ones. So, why do you keep it secret?

A lot of people don't talk about the fact they are a prepper simply because they are worried they will be stereotyped. This may happen - there is no doubt about that. But it isn't something you should let bother you! Preppers are often made fun of and people think they are stockpiling weapons and preparing for the sky to fall. While in some ways they are right, the people who are prepping are doing so to save themselves and their families from very real and possible scenarios. And who do you think people will turn to in times of crisis? The preppers, of course!

You would be surprised to learn how many preppers there truly are out there. Sometimes, people just need to be turned onto the world of prepping. When they realize that their neighbors next door, who go to work, take their kids to soccer and have backyard barbecues and are by all accounts "normal", it helps chip away at that stereotype. People can be perfectly normal citizens and still prepare their family to get through any disaster.

Many people *are* preppers and don't even realize it. We all have that friend or family member who keeps a few months worth of food supplies in a pantry. Ask them why they have so much food and they'll say things like "Oh, it was on sale" or "Oh, this way I don't have to go out shopping in the winter weather". They wouldn't call themselves a prepper, but they sure are acting like one!

There are many simple ways to let others know about your prepping habits, and to even get them involved. Start bringing up the idea of prepping in casual conversation with your neighbors or friends. Get a read on what they think. If they are open to discussing it, talk with them about how you can work together to prepare your homes and families. Picture your neighborhood or town after a catastrophic event. You are probably not a doctor, gardener, handyman and electrician. But, your neighbors and friends probably have different skills than you do. Combining your skills and relying on each other is one sure way you can ensure you will survive and prosper following a devastating event. Dividing up responsibilities like, hunting, manning a fire or keeping watch allows you to get the rest you need in order to stay healthy.

Community is human nature. We want to be able to talk to others about what we are dealing with and we want to bounce ideas off people who can give us a different perspective. By forming your community early on, you are setting yourself up for success. You are taking a divide and conquer approach to survival. If your children have other children to play with or talk with, you will all be a lot happier.

If you know your home isn't a good place to hunker down in, but your neighbor has a basement that would make an excellent retreat, you need to ask about bringing your family into the neighbor's basement. Talk about what you can bring to the table in skills, supplies and moral support. In many situations, it makes more sense to keep a few families together in order to conserve heat and resources.

Generally, people are going to be much more open to the idea of prepping if someone they know, respect, or care about brings it up. This is our duty as preppers. We can't let our friends and loved ones think that all preppers are a bunch of nutcases. We need to let them know that what they see on TV or read on the Internet isn't true about every prepper. That, deep down, prepping is about protecting yourself and your loved ones, and that it is most successful if you can get others involved. When people see it this way, they're a lot more open-minded and usually even ready to join in and help in whatever ways they can. If you keep your prepping a secret, you'll miss out on these opportunities to strengthen yourself, your family, and your future.

#3 - Preparing Mostly to Bug Out (Instead of Bugging In)

In the prepping world, you read and see a lot about bugging out or getting out of dodge when it hits the fan. Everyone is focused on packing the absolute best bug out bag, having multiple escape plans, safe houses, and meet up locations. Don't get me wrong: those are all good things to be thinking about and even preparing for. But focusing on that is missing the entire other half of the equation.

What if you can't leave your house? What if there is a severe storm or there is an army forcing you to hunker down in your home? Are you prepared to survive in your current location? One of the biggest misconceptions people have about preppers and prepping in general is that a bug out bag is the main component of prepping. There is this idea that as soon as you hear the first siren or hear of civil unrest, you grab your bag and start running. This is a dangerous belief!

A bug out bag is definitely worth devoting some effort to, but you need a contingency plan. The bug out bag *cannot* be your only plan. What if you really cannot leave your house? Honestly, if you didn't have to, would you really want to in the first place? Your home has all the creature comforts you could want. You can stockpile food, water, blankets and other emergency gear in your home without worrying if it will fit into your backpack. Wouldn't you feel a lot safer in the familiar confines of home, rather than out in the elements, on the run, not sure where you will end up every night. Depending on the situation that has caused a prepping event, many times staying at home is the much, much better choice.

The goal of preparing for anything is just that – a goal. You can't assume you will automatically leave your home and head out into the great blue yonder, no matter what. You need to prepare to bug in as well. Spend some time developing plans for either scenario. Ideally, if you can stay in your home, that should be your first option. This will take care of your need to find shelter and give you some time to evaluate the situation. It will also eliminate the line of foot and vehicle traffic that is likely exiting the city. Don't get too caught up in the excitement of bugging out. Sure it's fun to build a bug out bag and imagine yourself out in the wild, in the elements, building a fire and hunting your food. But think about it – is that *really* the most ideal situation? Definitely not. Take the time to evaluate the situation and choose the plan that is best for your family.

Focusing solely on bugging out can also leave you vulnerable, especially in extreme weather conditions. One of your first priorities when bugging out is finding shelter. It doesn't make a lot of sense to head out into a snowstorm or hurricane simply because you have been practicing and focusing on bugging out and your bug out bag is all ready. You will find that most plans involve both, hunkering down and bugging out. Depending on the situation, where you live, and what your secondary location looks like, you will likely need to hunker down and wait until it is safe to move or move and then hunker down. So don't focus all of your time, efforts, and money on bugging out now. Plan for both, prepare for both, stock items for both, and practice both. That way you'll be ready to survive, no matter what the situation.

#4 - Having a Lot of Gear (But Not Knowing How to Use It)

Did you spend some time surfing the net or trolling your local army surplus stores finding some really cool gear? You've narrowed down your choices, read all of the reviews, and thought that you absolutely needed this thing for your prepping? You probably read the packaging and decided each piece was definitely a necessity to your survival and you paid for it not truly understanding what it was. Maybe you reasoned that the packaging included the face of a dude who is famous for his survival skills so if his face is on it, it must be really good, right? Or you assume the pictures on the packaging are pretty self-explanatory and how hard could it really be to use it when the time comes?

This is a common and costly prepping mistake. Unfortunately, many preppers buy everything but the kitchen sink and shove it into their bug out bag or stock it in their basement with the rest of their emergency supplies. They then forget about it completely and it sits there gathering dust. Some of the gear can be very expensive. Some people assume that the price obviously reflects how valuable it is and it must be worth every penny if a famous dude wearing camo uses it. Big mistake! That isn't exactly true. In fact, there are plenty of marketing experts who are aware of the prepping movement and who are taking advantage of people's lack of knowledge and creating various doodads marketed for survival and making a boatload of cash. Sadly, many of the pieces of gear are completely unnecessary or make claims that are not entirely true. There are some tools that are nothing more than a glorified screwdriver but sell for the price of a small car.

Don't rush out and buy a bunch of gear and shove it in the basement or your bug out bag and forget about it. The most fancy, shiniest, and most expensive tools do not use themselves. Price does not necessarily reflect quality or usefulness. And, remember, you still have to know how to use all of that gear you are buying. Don't assume you will figure it out when the time comes. You don't have time to be learning anything new in a survival situation.

First off, stop buying single-use gear, whenever possible. Buy gear that serves many purposes and can be reused for multiple tasks. Do spend extra money buying a quality piece of gear rather than a cheap counterpart that will break after a couple of uses. Practice with it often in a variety of conditions. Try using it in the dark, when it is raining outside or when the wind is blowing. Professional basketball players don't show up on the court and assume a basketball is pretty self-explanatory and they don't need to actually mess with the ball until game day. You have to practice and get familiar with the quirks of your gear and how it works the best for you. Practice makes perfect is my prepping mantra and it should be yours too. Don't be the only member of your family who knows how to use the tools either. Give everyone a chance to practice and become familiar with the tools. You're all going to need to know how to use survival tools when the time comes, so the time to start practicing is now.

When you are practicing with your gear, you are going to become so familiar with using it that it will become second nature. This is what we want. You will know how far you can push it before it breaks. You will know it's little quirks and tips and tricks. It will also give you the opportunity to think of other uses for the tool. If you can eliminate a second tool from your bug out bag, you are making a little more room for an extra granola bar or bottle of water.

Do not make the mistake of more is better. More can get you killed. Having so much gear that you can't move freely because you are weighed down by a stuffed bug out bag or you can't find the tool you need in a hurry is a recipe for disaster. The motto for your prepping tools should be: simple and useful. Don't buy the newest gear just because you saw it on TV or read about it somewhere. Don't fall into the consumerism trap of thinking you *need* the newest gadget, when something you already have will do the same exact job. Know what tools you have. Know how to use the tools you have. Make sure your family or friends know how to use the tools. Stay away from buying flashy things just because they're new and shiny.

#5 - Storing All of Your Preps in the Same Place

You have heard the phrase, "Don't put all of your eggs into one basket." Well, in the world of prepping, we can translate that to say, "Don't put all your preps in one place." Don't load your basement with every bit of your supplies. What happens if your house is destroyed or your basement floods? All of your time, money and hard work will be for naught. Your food and lifeline will be gone. Don't put all of your gear in the garage – what if a fire strikes? Don't put everything in your bug out bag – what if that gets lost? You get the idea. Everything in one place is nothing but a recipe for disaster. And it's something that can be so easily avoided.

You want to spread the wealth, so to speak. Spread the gear. Spread the prep! You should have second options for just about everything, wherever possible. As part of your prepping plan, you should have a secondary location chosen for your family to bug out to in case your home is compromised. You will need to keep supplies in both locations. If you don't have a second home or cabin to retreat to, consider burying supplies in an area where you plan to bug out to or even around your backyard. Make sure you mark the area in a way you will notice, but others will not.

Keep gear in each one of your vehicles, in your desk drawer at work and along the route you would take to get from work to home in an emergency. This may sound like overkill, but you have to consider ALL the disasters that could occur and leave you and your family in a survival situation. You don't have to store a year's worth of food and water in every location. Simply put in a few bottles of water, a knife and a way to start fire. That is all you really need to get started on your survival journey.

If you are working with friends or neighbors, you may want to consider distributing supplies to their homes as well. This is risky, but if you trust the people, do it. You are probably safe putting things at your sister's, brother's or parent's house to use. If your family members are not on board with your prepping, think twice before putting your supplies in their home. You don't want them to borrow your food when they are making dinner or entertaining guests.

You also want to be careful storing your preps in one place in case your home is broken into by people intent on taking what you have. If you have everything in one place like your pantry or basement, looters are going to take it all. By placing preps throughout your home in not-so-obvious places, you are ensuring you will have something left if you are robbed. Looters are not going to waste a lot of time searching your home top to bottom. If they find a stash of food in the pantry, they are going to assume that is it and move on. Little do they know you have a couple boxes in the garage labeled "Christmas decorations" that are actually filled with water and food.

Too often, people will spend a whole lot of time, money, and effort building up a great prep. They'll load it up with food, water, and all other kinds of necessary supplies. They go through all of that trouble, only to store it all in one, single location. Big mistake! Don't do that to yourself. Don't waste your prepping efforts by not having a backup location. You've done everything else right up to this point, so do the simple, smart thing, and spread your prep around. It doesn't have to be spread into ten different places or intricately buried around town with a treasure map. Keep it simple, but keep it separated. You'll thank yourself later.

#6 - Not Rotating Your Food Supplies

If you have been adding food to your emergency food storage for several months already, you may be guilty of this. It's something simple but something that a lot of people can easily overlook. You have to rotate your food! If the world around you does come crashing in and you are forced to rely on that food you have been storing, what will you do when you discover it is spoiled? Spoiled to the point it would be potentially deadly to eat? All that work for naught. Look – grocery stores rotate food. Restaurants rotate food. So why wouldn't you?

There is a rule you must follow when you are building up your food storage—FIFO. FIFO stands for first in, first out. When you are adding new cans or other food to your shelves, pull the old stuff forward and put the new stuff in back. Take the time to check the condition of the cans, boxes and bags of food you have on your shelf. Check the expiration dates. If something is out of date, pull it out of your food storage and replace it with a fresh item. If something is coming really close to being out of date, pull it and use it for dinner. You can replace it with a fresh one and still get use out of the old one before it spoils. Best of both worlds.

Technically, a best by date means just that. It's a date that, ideally, the food is most fresh, or best used by. The box of crackers with a best by date is a guideline. If you open it up after the best by date, you are probably going to discover the crackers are stale. They are safe to eat, but they are just not as great a quality as they would have been before that date. The dates on your food are put there by the manufacturers as a quality control mechanism and as a way to cover their own behinds. They don't want to sell food that is past its prime. It is, however, just a guideline, and not a hard and fast rule.

Although you can technically eat most food that has gone past its expiration date, you do need to be careful. Look for signs the food is spoiled. Cans of food that are leaking, bulging or have a nasty odor when you open them up should never be consumed. Do your best to keep your food stores fresh by pulling out food that is close to its expiration and using it in your daily meals. Replace what you took and you will ensure you are keeping a fresh supply of food. You never know when disaster will strike so you want to stay on top of the rotation. Commit to checking your food storage at least once a month. If it helps, keep a running inventory on a spreadsheet. Print off the spreadsheet and keep it in your purse or wallet. The next time you go to the grocery store, you will know what supplies are running low or are close to expiring. This can help you avoid having 20 cans of corn and a single can of green beans on hand.

Take care in choosing storage spaces that are conducive to long shelf lives. Avoid extreme heat or cold, moisture and direct sunlight. Do your best to manage pests to keep them from getting in and spoiling your food. Invest in 5-gallon food grade buckets and Mylar bags. You can extend the shelf life of things like dried grains and beans and pastas for years when you seal the food in Mylar bags.

Use common sense when rotating and stocking your pantry. Obviously some things are going to have a much shorter shelf life than others. If you have any baked products, dairy, refrigerated meats or produce, those are going to go bad much more quickly than canned goods, dried goods, jerky, or things of that nature. Rotate their stocks more often and use the older goods more frequently.

This is a task that you can really get your whole family involved in. Some kids don't like certain prepping tasks, but some really love dealing with food and the pantry. Make it into a fun game. Get a clipboard and some paper and teach them how to make a log of the pantry items, with bought dates, best-by dates, used dates, and things such as that. Have one of their chores be checking the pantry, keeping an eye on dates and suggesting which items you should use, which items you need to buy more of, and which items need to be rotated. This will really help them feel involved in the family prepping process and is a great way to teach them skills that will help in all areas of their lives. Which leads us to the next common mistake that preppers make…

#7 - Not Getting the Entire Family Involved

You don't have to prep alone. In fact, you *shouldn't* be prepping alone. Not if you have a family. Do not try to be the hero in your family. Every person in your family should be involved in your prepping. You don't have to send the kids to the grocery store to buy a bunch of canned food for your food storage, but you do need to have them help you do the rotation and stock the shelves. They need to know where the food is and what they should eat just in case you are not there when things go sideways.

It is a good idea to delegate various tasks to help take some of the workload off you while getting the family involved. You need every hand to help out when things go bad. Your kids, wife, husband or whatever will all play a vital role in the ultimate survival of the whole family. Talk with your children about what they need to do if they hear the sirens go off or if you call them and tell them it's time. You don't want to spend precious minutes explaining what needs to happen in the real event. Run drills to help them remember what it is they are supposed to do when you sound the alarm. This allows you to focus on doing other things because you know the rest of the family is doing what they are supposed to. Working together as a team ups your odds for survival tremendously.

If you have nearby relatives, get them involved too. It will be an all hands on deck situation when the real situation unfolds. Work together to create plans for bugging out, bugging in and what escape routes you will use. Each family member needs to know what to do. You cannot be with them every second of the day. Not telling them what to do, where to go or what gear to use is setting them up for failure. They may grumble a bit and chalk your desire for them to be involved as crazy, but that crazy just may save their lives. Explain to them why you are prepping, why you are practicing, and why they need to be involved. You don't need to scare them, but they do need to understand the importance of it and how they fit into the overall survival plan.

You also have to plan for the worst. If you are incapacitated, you are going to be relying on your family to pick up the slack. What if you have to leave out of town and the world falls apart while you are hundreds of miles away from your family? They have to know what to do and where to find the supplies you have been building up.

You also need to think of the future. Depending on the severity of the crisis, you could be living on your wits and skill for a year or more. Your family will feel better if they are prepared to live without running water or electricity. If they are thrust into the situation without a clue as to how they will survive, it will wreak havoc on their mental health. Survival is just as much mental as it is physical. If they panic or give up, they will surely fall victim to the catastrophe.

You can help eliminate the fear of living in a different world by training and preparing them for doing things a little differently. They will not be as scared and will be more capable of helping out. It will give them a purpose and a feeling of accomplishment. You don't want them sitting around fretting over their circumstances.

Give them the tools they need to thrive. Remember: the family that preps together, survives together!

#8 - Not Having the Skills to Live Sustainability

Another huge mistake preppers make is by loading up on food and water and kicking back, waiting for the sky to fall. Without doing anything else. So, what if the catastrophic event that happens is so severe that the world will take several years to right itself? Do those preppers have enough food and water on hand to last three years? Not likely. Do they have the skills to survive once their current stash runs out? Even less likely. Most preppers think they have enough food and water to last them a year when, in fact, they only have enough to last about six months. So, they survived the first six months following a disaster, now what?

You cannot assume you have stored enough to get you by indefinitely. An emergency food storage is only half the battle. It's meant for emergencies, not long-term survival of years or more. You have to be prepared for the almost unthinkable event that may wipe out your food storage before you ever get the chance to use it or for an event that lasts a whole lot longer than you had originally prepped for.

You need to learn some valuable skills that will keep you alive when the food runs out. Take the time to learn and practice how to hunt, fish and forage. The vast majority of the population has no idea how to do any of these things. If you learn even one of them, you'll be at a much greater advantage when the time comes for you to use those skills. You also need to try your hand at gardening, if you have never done so in the past. It can seem intimidating at first, but if you learn the basics, you'll find that it's not too difficult to grow enough food to supplement your pantry at least. Depending on your climate, you can grow an amazingly large variety of fruits, vegetables, tubers, and more. Think about cities you have lived in or where you live now – how many people actually have a garden? How far ahead of the pack would you be if you had a garden and knew how to use it?

If you don't have a big yard or live in an apartment, you can still grow things in containers. Read up about patio gardening and you'll find a whole wealth of information to get you started. Just on a balcony or deck alone, you can grow all kinds of lettuce, tomatoes, peas, and more. Don't forget to add heirloom seeds to your preps. You have to start somewhere. Along with typical summer gardening, you will want to learn how to grow food in the winter months as well, if your climate demands it. Look into what it takes to make a greenhouse out of scraps laying around the house. Odds are that you will already have a lot of the necessary material or could easily obtain it. Cold frames are another option you will want to read about. This ensures you have a source of food all year round. You should take up gardening and hunting even if you have food on hand to supplement your supplies. Don't wait to figure it out when the food runs out.

Hunting doesn't necessarily require you to use a gun. If you are relying on a gun to hunt game, you need to have extra ammunition on hand. Plus, you better practice your shot – it's not as easy as it looks. Shooting a running animal is difficult. Many experts will advise you leave the big game alone and focus your efforts on small animals that tend to be more abundant and a lot easier to procure. You will want to learn how to build traps and snares and how to fish without the luxury of a fancy rod and reel. You cannot survive on meat alone and will need to learn what plants are safe to eat. There are hundreds of edibles that are often viewed as weeds in today's world. Those weeds may just keep you alive someday. It would be a good idea to include a book of edible plants in your emergency preps. There are a lot of lookalike plants out there. Some are toxic. Better safe than sorry. The time to start studying is now! Get the whole family involved and you can make it fun. Spot the edible plant. Build a trap together. Learn to love fishing as a group. These are all skills that will help you survive and thrive in any catastrophic event.

Last, but certainly not least, you also need to know how to find water and then clean the water to make it safe to drink. You can (and should) add purifying tablets to your pantry. They're relatively cheap, extremely useful, and may just save your life. Eventually, though, even those will run out, if the survival event stretches on longer than you had imagined. Try to plan a safe house near freshwater, if at all possible. If you own land, build up a well or two. These are the types of investments that will pay off far into the future.

Read up on how to create catchment systems that allow you to catch rainwater instead of journeying out into the forest or urban areas to find water. Everyone will have the same plan and needs and it may get dangerous if you have to go out searching for water. If you can avoid this situation, you should plan now to be able to do so. Water is an absolute necessity and should be your biggest concern. You don't want to wake up one day and realize you have just drunk your last bottle of water and you don't have a clue as to where to find more. Plan early, plan often, plan now!

#9 - Always Believing the 'Experts' (Hint…Don't Do It!)

This is a tough one for many people. They watch TV or read books or blog and think that everyone they come across knows what they are talking about. But not every survival expert is really a survival expert (shocking, I know!). Always read carefully and realize who the source of the information is. Is it someone looking to sell you something? Someone who wants you to watch a certain TV show?

The simple fact is that a lot of these so-called experts make prepping a lot more complicated, and expensive, then it really needs to be. You don't have to have a bunch of gear to survive. You don't have to have 5-years worth of expensive freeze-dried food sitting on your shelf to ensure survival. You don't need the latest 99-in-1 tool which, oh, by the way, costs only $199!

There are always going to people trying to sell you stuff you don't need. It may not all be snake oil, but you certainly don't need a gold-plated multi-functional tool with your engraved initials. Keep it simple and you will be better off. Getting a bunch of complicated fancy gear is more dangerous than only having a single knife. The fancier the gear is, the bigger the learning curve and the more things that can go wrong with it. You will also develop a false sense of security if you surround yourself with all of the latest gadgets. You may assume that all is good because you have that cool tool that the expert said you needed. When that tool is lost or it fails, you are in big trouble. You will not have studied or practiced what to do without that tool, and you'll be paying for it, big time.

It isn't like there is a universal test that survivalists take to become an expert. Anybody can claim to be an expert without ever having stepped food in the forest or without actually starting a fire from nothing more than a couple of sticks. The term expert is used rather loosely. Use your common sense when you are reading or listening to somebody explain how to survive a disaster. Are they speaking from experience? Are they saying believable things? Are they trying to sell you something at the end of the day (and if so, run!).

Don't get caught up in a lot of hype. Most of the gadgets that are marketed towards preppers can be made with your own two hands for a fraction of the price. Or you can find a much cheaper, just as effective replacement. You don't have to spend a lot of money on gadgets and gizmos. You don't have to have specific brands of gear or a bunch of fancy kitchen tools to cook your meals. When you see a particular piece of gear that looks promising, take some time to research it. Read comments and reviews from others who have actually tried it. You don't want all the marketing hype. You want real information from real people who have used the tool or have come up with cheaper alternatives that are just as effective.

Buying food and gear should be your priority. If you can spend $20 on a bunch of food or $20 on a single tool that you may use once or twice, you have to consider which one will get you the most bang for your buck. Above all, remember: the tools and gadgets you buy are only as good as the user behind them…which will be you! Spend the time to learn your tools and you will be so much more effective with them than if you had just bought the newest, most expensive, flashiest gear!

#10 – Forgetting to Have Backups for Your Backups

What's the prepper's mantra? Always Be Prepared. I'll add to that: Always Be Prepared…and then prepare some more! We have no way of what's going to happen in the future. All we can do is plan to the best of our abilities. And that means having multiple plans. You can never have too much food or water. You can never have too many escape routes. Too many emergency contacts. Too many safe houses. You can never prepare too much. One of the main reasons we prep is because we want to prepare for almost any and everything. You cannot possibly predict what will happen in the future, of course. Therefore, you must have a plan A, B, C and so on. For every plan you come up with, you must have an option just in case something goes wrong. If you are planning on escaping the city via the highway and the highway becomes blocked, you need an alternative route. If the back road you planned on using is filled with aggressive people, you need another route and so on.

If your food storage is somehow destroyed, stolen or you can't get to it, you need to have backups in another location. There are so many different possible scenarios, it is almost impossible to predict every eventuality. You have to do your best to back up each one of your back ups. If you are not prepared with a contingency plan, you have to be ready to improvise.

Consider your bug out bag. Maybe you packed a box of waterproof matches as a way to get a fire going. Somewhere along the way, the matches fell out of your pack. Your back up plan would be your flint rod. If that is gone, then you must be prepared to make a bow drill. Prepare, prepare, prepare! Never assume everything will go according to plan or like you practiced. In reality, nothing ever goes exactly as you had trained for. Being prepared and being able to improvise is your best bet at making it through a disaster.

If you have decided to stock up on waterproof matches as your method of starting a fire, back it up with flint rod and steel. Back that up with a lighter. Back up your lighter with some steel wool and a battery. Lastly, learn how to make a bow drill. Fire is life. You can't afford not to have a backup plan when the first few options fail.

A great way to brainstorm for potential ideas that you may have missed is to get your entire family involved. Make it a fun game. Ask a question, such as: How do we get to Grandma's house if the freeway is closed? Let your children or spouse ponder it and see what they come up with. Oftentimes, they will come up with a solution that you may not have even considered. So not only is it a useful exercise, but it can be quite fun as well. It helps get everyone thinking one or two steps ahead, and that is exactly the mentality that will help you all survive when it comes down to it.

Conclusion

Prepping doesn't have to be complicated. You don't need to follow a bunch of rules or advice from so-called 'experts' on TV. What you *do* need to do is tailor your prepping for *you* and your specific experience. Hopefully now that you are aware of these 10 Prepping Mistakes that most people make, at some point, you can avoid them completely. If you can steer clear of these common pitfalls, you will already be far ahead of the pack with your prepping habits. Not only that, but you'll save time, money, and energy – all things that will be better spent on prepping activities that are actually helpful to you!

Your prepping will constantly be evolving with changes in your family, changes in your neighborhood and most importantly, changes in the current events of the world, of the country, of the state, and of your surroundings. Go with the flow and do your best to avoid making one of these costly mistakes. Constantly evaluate your preps and work to make them better. You can always improve on things. Hone your skills and be prepared. It the day never comes that you have to use your preps, count yourself fortunate, but make sure that you and your family are prepared to deal with any event that may happen in your lifetime. Pass on and share your wisdom, and keep the prepping tradition alive and well. You and your family will be much better off for it.

Stay calm. Stay in control. Stay ahead of the game. Follow these tips and avoid the mistakes above, and you will be well on your way.

Good luck, fellow Preppers!

*****

The Grid Down Prepper

Introduction

Have you ever dealt with a power outage? Maybe it lasted for only a few hours or maybe all day. It was probably frustrating, but not that big of a concern because you knew it would be back up soon. What would you do if the power grid went down for an extended period of time? Would you know how to survive? To thrive?

It is almost impossible to think of our lives without electricity. Everything we do is somehow connected to the power grid. Imagine your morning routine for a minute. You get up, probably turn on the radio or television to hear the news for the day. Maybe you go for your phone, which has been charging in the electrical plug-in all night. Turn on the coffee maker before jumping in a hot shower. Before you head out the door, you grab a couple waffles out of the freezer and pop them in the toaster. You go to work, you use computers, the elevator and lights. Do you see where this is going? We, as a society living in a very modern world, are completely reliant upon electricity. We can't eat breakfast, brush our teeth or entertain ourselves without electricity. And most of us don't ever give it a second thought.

Though we may never even think about it, the possibility of the power grid failing is very real. Choosing to put your head in the sand and ignore all of the warning signs isn't helpful. Just because we are used to something and it seems like it has always been there, we cannot ignore the fact that the possibility exists. The government knows the power grid can and likely will fail at some point. They run drills with law enforcement, EMS and even the military on how to handle such a situation. Many people don't fully understand how widespread a power grid failure would be.

Minor power outages tend to affect only certain parts of the city, one or two blocks, leaving some stores open for business. Most people, therefore, see these as small inconveniences, tiny little blips in an otherwise perfectly-working system. But that is simply not the case! If the power grid goes down, nothing about our daily lives would be "normal". Things would not just continue to go along, as if nothing had happened. A major grid failure would paralyze an entire region, effecting hundreds of thousands, possibly millions of people. If the entire U.S. system goes down – well, you can start to imagine the chaos and mayhem an event of that size would cause.

Everything we do involves electricity. It touches nearly every aspect of our modern world. And it's not just contained to our lives at home or inside buildings. Think outside the four walls of your home for a minute. Check out some of the things from the following list and then you will see just how serious a power grid failure would be.

- Gas pumps wouldn't work
- Cash registers wouldn't work and safes wouldn't be able to be opened
- Credit card machines wouldn't work
- ATM machines would be down

- Banks would be shut down

- Grocery stores would be unable to sell you food

- Businesses without backup generators would close—those that had generators will only have the gas on hand to run the generators

- Traffic lights would stop

- Subways and rail systems would stop

- Restaurants would be unable to cook or serve food

- Hospitals and clinics would not have access to electronic patient records, which would make healthcare a serious concern

And that's just a start. This is why a power grid failure would be devastating. Commerce would be halted, which means you wouldn't be able to work and earn a paycheck. The money you have on hand when the power grid fails is all you have to get by on. The modern world, as we know it, would grind to a halt. It is a serious situation that deserves attention. Even some of the most-seasoned preppers only prepare for one event, say, a governmental collapse or a natural disaster. A power grid failure is often one of the least-prepared for events. But now that you know how serious it can get, you can start working on a plan. Preparing to ride out a grid failure is your best hope. If you are prepared to survive, and thrive, without electricity, you will be better off than 99.9% of the population. And that's what it's all about – being prepared!

So, let's get started.

Possible Causes of the Grid going down

Believe it or not, there are actually several different reasons the power grid could fail. It would be easier to believe that it couldn't happen if there was only a single, far-fetched reason. Unfortunately, there are plenty of very real scenarios that could leave us all sitting in the dark for days, weeks and possibly even months. The following are some of the most likely causes of a grid failure, though they are, for sure, not the only possibilities.

Natural disaster

This one is not hard to believe for most people, when you really start to talk to them about the grid going down. Many people have even experienced it themselves, on much smaller levels. Natural disasters are a common occurrence these days. Things like hurricanes, tornadoes, blizzards, and earthquakes can easily take out a power grid. We have seen it happen several times in the past couple of years, all over the United States and Europe. A severe storm or extremely strong weather is always a possibility. Depending on the severity of the disaster and the area that was hit, a power outage could affect millions of people.

Remember when New Orleans was left in the dark for days? Or, more recently, we saw Hurricane Sandy cripple New York City. Do you remember how people responded to such weather events? They panicked. They didn't know what to do. People were forced into darkness for several days. In the hours and days before Sandy hit, stores were wiped out of things like water, bread and flashlights.

Even those minor preps did very little to help those who were left without power for several weeks. And this was with advanced warning!

Things like earthquakes, on the other hand, give no warning. We know certain areas are due for a strong earthquake, but nobody knows when it will strike. Can you imagine the chaos and panic that would ensue if a major earthquake hits San Francisco again (like it is predicted to)? If people have a hard time prepping and surviving with advanced warnings even, then they have no hope of making it through an unplanned, unannounced natural disaster such as an earthquake.

War (foreign or domestic)

We have been very fortunate not to have a foreign war on our soil in the past couple hundred years. Yes, we have had terrorist attacks. However, those are typical fairly localized and do not disrupt the grid in any meaningful way. Many of us would not be prepared for an invasion by a foreign army or a terrorist attack on the national power grid. If a bomb was dropped that took out a power grid, we would suffer greatly. In fact, a small nuclear bomb detonated way above the atmosphere, it would create an electromagnetic pulse that would paralyze the power grid. The nuclear fallout would be nothing compared to the failed power grid.

It doesn't only have to be an attack from a foreign government. There are plenty of folks right here in the country who are willing to make war or who are actively trying to disrupt our daily lives. Many are predicting we are headed for another civil war of sorts. If that happens, the power grid would be at risk. It would likely be one of the first things targeted because it would result in so much damage.

In the event of a war or a terrorist attack on the power grid system, who knows how long it would take to get back to 'normal'. The government and armed forces will be busy trying to take care of the immediate armed threat. Average citizens will be at home, scared to death. Who will fix the power grid? How long will it take? We have no way of knowing, so the only thing we can is prepare to live without electricity for as long as it may take.

Terrorism (foreign or domestic)

An act of terror doesn't always come in the form of a bomb or some other equally horrible attack. A single computer virus that was programmed to take out our power grid is a real possibility. There have been plenty of rumors this type of attack is imminent. The attack could come from the outside or on our own soil. Recently, several power stations in California were shot out. The power company was able to divert power to other transformers and prevent a widespread outage, but many are concerned this one attack was a dry run. If there was a coordinated attack on a dozen or more stations throughout an area, it would cause widespread power outages. It would take weeks for the power company to repair the transformers and restore power. That is assuming the rest of the power grid did not come under attack.

Action by our government or outside players

Our government may choose to shut down portions of the power grid for numerous reasons. If there is civil unrest and rioting that is causing serious damage, the government may opt to cut the power to an area until order can be restored. We've seen this tactic used in isolated neighborhoods already, but it could just as easily be used in entire cities, regions, even states. Military Law could be imposed that would limit the amount of power delivered to a particular area. If power was in short supply due to a natural disaster, act of war, or simply because the grid is overtaxed, the government could choose to limit power and divert it as they see fit.

We've already seen rolling blackouts in parts of the country, so it's not too far-fetched to imagine the government trying this technique across the entire country, in greater and greater time periods, leaving us with no choice but to try and survive without electricity until they decide to restore it for us. That is a situation we are prepping to avoid – we want to be able to survive and thrive without electricity and to not be dependent on the government, or anyone else.

Experts agree that our power infrastructure is extremely vulnerable to a cyber or physical attack. We've seen cyber terrorists and hackers already easily steal personal data from hundreds of thousands of Americans through coordinated online attacks. It's not a big stretch to see them attack another portion of the U.S. through online attacks. Many of the power grids across America are extremely old and outdated. They might have little to no digital security and may be particularly vulnerable to cyber attacks. The government recognizes this vulnerability and has been working behind the scenes to prepare for the ultimate take down of the grid. Communications during a grid failure will be restricted, so the government is coordinating their reaction with several agencies in order to institute protocol if and when the grid fails.

What may happen if the Grid Collapses

Now that you see just how possible it is for the grid to collapse, let's get into what could actually happen in the midst of the grid collapse. As we discussed earlier, our entire lives center around electricity. If you don't have a car charger for your cell phone, laptop or tablet, it won't be long before those are rendered useless. Sitting in a dark, quiet house for a couple hours is nothing compared to going days on end with no electricity. It's not something that most of us are used to. If you are unable to work and the kids can't go to school, it won't be long before you start climbing the walls! We have become so accustomed to being plugged in that we struggle to get through the day without using our favorite appliances and devices. When people are unplugged with no warning, they are going to struggle and tensions are going to rise quickly.

The average person or family will be completely lost with the most mundane tasks, such as how to eat, bathe and even keep themselves and their surroundings safe and clean. Your hot water tank would be useless. Most people wouldn't know how to start a fire to cook with and would be forced to eat cold goods or boxed items like crackers and cookies. Washing your hands would have to be done with cold water because you couldn't even heat water on the stove. Think back again to Hurricane Katrina and Hurricane Sandy. These events first took the country by surprise. Yes, people knew the storms were coming, but even then they were not prepared to deal with a failed power grid and the destruction of the hurricane-force winds. With Hurricane Sandy, New York knew it was coming at least a week in advance and most people thought they were prepared, with families buying a couple loaves of bread and a pack of batteries for their flashlights. They were in for a big, nasty surprise when the storm left many areas of the city in the dark for days. We saw how much chaos and havoc that caused. Now imagine that on a larger, national scale.

After these big storms, we saw that it wasn't long before people were out of food, batteries and clean drinking water. The 3-day supply the government recommends is typically not enough and those people learned that the hard way. Some people were prepared with canned food and freeze-dried packs of food. Did they remember to factor in the extra water needed to rehydrate the food or a manual can opener to open the canned food?

Most people would be completely thrown off of their normal lives if the power were to go down for an extended period of time. Kids would likely suffer the worst. They have been brought up in a technical age where most of their toys are powered by electricity or batteries. They are used to watching television and playing video games. Adults are used to being able to surf the Internet while watching television. It can leave a person feeling a little lost when their routines are severely interrupted. You would seriously stand in your kitchen and feel like you were in a foreign land. No microwave, no stove and no refrigerator. Whatever was in your pantry would be what you had for dinner. You couldn't run through the drive-thru anywhere or go out to eat because you don't have power at home. They wouldn't have power either. So, what would you do?

The upheaval in typical routine would leave many people struggling to the point they would do things they wouldn't normally do. If a person was left in the dark without any food, water, or a way to light their home, they may resort to looting store shelves. Imagine if the kids are crying and begging you for food. You would do just about anything to take care of your family. People figure if others are looting the stores, you jumping in and grabbing a few supplies won't make a difference. We can see how this would quickly get out of control.

Lawlessness would make the streets unsafe. That means people would be forced to hole up in their homes and wait for help. Again, refer back to the chaos following Hurricane Katrina. The city of New Orleans was nearly destroyed by the looting and destructing by disgruntled citizens. Sure, the hurricane caused plenty of damage, but it was the days following the storm that made it unsafe to be outside. Can you imagine this happening in your town? If not, you should. It can, and may, happen in any town across the United States. So, how can you prepare?

How to prepare for limited access to running water

One of the biggest concerns you should have following a collapse of the power grid is water. Obviously, we all need water to survive. It's the most important thing we need to secure. Yet, for most people, water security means buying a case of bottled water and calling it a day. This isn't good enough!

When the grid goes down, your tap water would no longer be safe to drink. Without a filtering system at the water sanitation department, the water coming through your tap would be unclean and, oftentimes, harmful to drink. Eventually, the water would dry up without pumps to pump it to your home. Stores will run out of bottled water quickly as panic sets in and people rush out to buy up as much water as they can.

You need to be ahead of this rush. You need water to survive. That is a given. In fact, you need at least a gallon of water per day for each member of your family. If you have pets, factor in another gallon of water. You cannot live more than a couple of days without water. Expert survivalists put the magic number as 3 days, but you would be feeling pretty rotten by day two without water.

You must be prepared to take care of your water situation immediately following the power grid failing. If you happen to be home, fill your bathtub with water, fill every available pot with water and disconnect the water heater. The water in the tank will be a backup supply, but you don't want contaminated water from the outside coming in. You will have a good supply to start with, but you need to be prepared to restock your water supply, and to do so quickly.

How to Find Water

If you don't have enough water stored in your home, you are going to need to track some down. Stores will be crazy with mad rushes of people looking to buy every last bottle of water. You'll want to avoid that madness. One way you can prepare for this eventuality is by getting a map or taking a walk or drive today to find the closest body of water. Do some scouting of your nearby surroundings and find one or two streams, rivers, or lakes. Walking the route is a good idea so you can get familiar with the path and learn how long it takes you to make it to the water. Again, lakes, streams, rivers and ponds are all options, so keep an eye out for any of them. Yes, pond water may seem nasty, but you can drink it in a pinch after purifying it, which we will discuss in the next section.

If you have bugged out to a second location after a grid collapse, you may not be as familiar with the area. In this case, one of the easiest ways to spot water is look for lots of green vegetation. Green signifies water is somewhere nearby. You can also look for animal tracks or look for birds flying over an area. The animals will lead you to water. Bees also tend to fly towards water. Certain trees are indicators of a steady supply of water as well. Cypress, water oak and river birch will only grow near water.

If you are in an arid area, you can dig, but this should only be done if you know that the water is relatively close to the surface.

Digging is a huge tax on your energy and uses a lot of calories. If you are already on the edge of dehydration, digging with little hope of finding water can be dangerous.

Once you have found a source of water, mark it on your maps. Make sure everyone in your family or surviving party knows where the water source is, and where a backup water source is. Before any major event happens, spend a few weekends practicing how you will get to your water sources. Take turns with different members of your family or party leading the way, so that you make sure everyone knows what to do when the real event happens.

How to Disinfect/Purify Water

Once you have found your water, DON'T DRINK IT! It will be difficult to resist taking just a little sip as you transport your water back home, but you absolutely must not drink it until you know it's safe. You must assume that any water you collect is unsafe to drink. Consider the number of animals that are drinking from the same water source. Animals like to stand in the water when they are drinking and when nature calls, they do their business in that water. Humans are not immune from this either. Water in the open usually contains a variety of dangerous bacteria and viruses that can make a human incredibly sick. The viruses are in the fecal matter of humans and animals and contaminate the water supply. Things like ecoli and giardia can wreak havoc on your digestive system resulting in dehydration or even death. You simply cannot risk drinking water without purifying it.

So how do you ensure the water is safe to drink? The easiest option is to use purification tablets. You will want to load up on several bottles of these. They are typically sold 30 to a bottle. Each tablet will usually purify a quart of water. You need a gallon of water per day per person, so that means a minimum of 4 tablets a day. Stock up on these now. They have a fairly long shelf life, so you can feel comfortable buying as many as you think you'll need. And then, buy a few more. This is one thing you can never have too many of.

Another option for purifying water is to boil it, but this could prove problematic in a world without electricity. If you can build a fire (which you should learn how to do!), then you can simply boil the water over a fire. This is a long-term, sustainable solution and, maybe not unsurprisingly, a skill that 99% of the population does not have. So if you can start a fire and boil your water, you'll be way ahead of the game.

The water only needs to boil a maximum of three minutes. Technically, the first bubble will kill all the microorganisms. Letting it boil longer is a waste of fuel and water lost by evaporation. Adding a few drops of standard household bleach is an option. It is very inexpensive and you only need a 1/4 teaspoon to purify a gallon of water. If the water is particularly cloudy, you may want to increase that to a 1/2 teaspoon. Keep in mind that household bleach has a shelf life of about 6 months before it starts to lose potency.

How to Filter Water

Filtering water is an option, but it is important to note that there are great differences in filters. You need to pay a little more and buy a filter with a .10 micron level of filtering. This is the smallest pore possible and will remove a majority of viruses. If you're relying on filters for your water, you need to get the smallest pores possible.

However, filters shouldn't be used as the only means of cleaning your drinking water. It is best to purify your water and then filter it to make it taste better. In a pinch, you could rely on your filter alone, but it is far from an ideal solution. Run the water through the filter several times to try and get rid of as many microorganisms as possible. If you don't have an actual filter, charcoal from a fire could also be used in combination with rocks and leaves. This is another last-resort type of filtration system, but it is certainly better than not filtering at all.

How to Store Water

You could save yourself a lot of trouble by storing water to drink in case of a grid failure. This will eliminate the need to purify your water or go out searching for it when it could be dangerous to do so. The most obvious choice for storing water is by buying cases of bottled water. This is great for a short-term grid failure situation, but for long-term, it wouldn't be feasible or very affordable. You would have to store about 1.5 cases per day for a family of 4. Assume your power is out for a week and you would need about 11 cases of bottled water. It is a bit of a space and money hog, and not really sustainable for any long-term planning situations.

Another option is to buy a few of the 5-gallon containers. These are made of a sturdy plastic and will store for years. They can be a bit bulky and heavy, so they are not easy to transport or to take with you if you need to bug out. But they can be a nice option if you know you are staying put.

If you have the space at home, look into buying a small water wall. These are square containers that are designed to stack on top of each other. Each container has a spout that makes it easy for you to get a small drink of water. These are a bit easier to store, as they save some space, and with the spout, they are much easier for everyone in the family to learn to use, young and old.

Another option that many people often don't think about is to bottle your own water. However, DO NOT use old milk jugs. The plastic is flimsy and it will break down in a matter of months. Juice containers and 2-liter soda bottles will work. Fill the water from your tap and add a drop of bleach. You will need to rotate your own bottled water supply about every six months, to ensure you have fresh, drinkable water when you need it. If the power goes out and you have "old" water on hand, you could purify it with more bleach or purification tablets to make it safe to drink.

Another idea is to consider investing in rain barrels that are set outside your home. You can store 50 gallons of water in a single barrel and the water is free. You can make your own barrel or buy one at Home Depot. You, of course, have to keep an eye out to ensure that nothing else gets in your barrel and the water is maintained in a safe, clean environment. But if you have the land

and you live in an area of the country that gets enough rain precipitation, rain barrels are a really great solution to water storage.

Sanitation

Staying clean and sanitary in a grid down situation will be a challenge. It's not something that most people think about, but in a long-term survival situation, sanitation can mean the difference between life and death. You can't afford to get sick due to improper sanitation. It is of the utmost importance you keep your home and body free of excess bacteria and germs. When the water isn't running and the toilets aren't flushing, it is a recipe for disaster. Years ago, when a city was left without water, people took to using the bathroom outside and the streets were lined with human fecal matter. It isn't just gross, it is deadly. There are far too many viruses passed through contact with fecal matter. So if you don't pay close attention to sanitation, you're just inviting yourself and your family to get sick and to spread the disease amongst each other. We need to avoid this! So, how to keep clean?

Toilets/Latrines

This may not be your favorite subject, and certainly your children or spouse may not want to think or talk about it, but you are going to have to come up with a way to use the toilet without contaminating your house or yard. There are a few options you have. What you choose to go with will depend on where you live and the weather.

Digging holes is one way to make sure you are taking care of business in a way that won't make anybody sick or stink up the area. It's probably the oldest sanitation method in the book, but it still works to this day, when done correctly. First, simply dig a hole, about six inches deep and do your deed. Fill the hole in. If you are in an area where animals are running around, put a rock or log over the area. You don't want them digging it up. If you have several people in the home, you can dig a bigger trench. Each time somebody uses the bathroom, fill in that section with dirt, working your way down the trench. It's not pleasant, but it will keep all the waste in one location, and covered, which is important.

If going outside isn't really an option, due to weather, or you live in an urban area, or for any other reason, you could line a 5-gallon bucket with a heavy-duty trash bag. A lid will help reduce the odor in between uses. Don't let the bag get overly full. It is a very good idea to double line the bucket. When you need to empty the bucket, take it as far from your home or any areas where people are as possible. Carry the entire bucket outside. Tie the bag off and bury it, if possible. If you don't have a bucket, you could use garbage bags and do the same thing. It's not pretty, but keeping yourself and your living space sanitary is the primary concern.

One more tip: If you are using the bathroom outside, make sure you are at least 200 feet from any water source. You don't want to contaminate the water!

Hand Washing

You need to do your best to wash your hands after using the bathroom, handling garbage or working outside. Of course, you should always be doing this, but in a grid down event, it's going to be even more necessary! Good hand washing will help prevent germs that could make you incredibly ill at a time you really can't afford it. It will also stop germs from spreading amongst your family or anyone else you are surviving with.

While you probably won't have hot water, you can still make do. Put the soap on your hands and work it in. Pour water over your hands to rinse the soap off. Don't use a universal bowl for everybody to wash their hands in. This is just putting all the germs, viruses and bacteria into one place. Do not reuse the water that you run over your hands. Use hand sanitizer after washing and in between washings to try and keep your hands as clean as possible. This is something you can stock up on early, as it has a very long shelf life. Get into the habit of washing hands or using sanitizer after using the restroom, before and after cooking and eating, after venturing outside, and similar situations. This will be an important habit for you and your family to carry on after a grid down event.

Dishes/Clothes

If you don't have disposable cutlery and dishes on hand, you are going to need to wash your dishes after each use. Of course, if you can find ways to eat without having to use dishes, that is equally as desirable. You must use potable water or water that has been purified at least. Don't use the water from the river or stream or pond. Again, those viruses and bacteria will cling to your dishes and end up making you sick. Even after washing, you would be left with bacteria from the dirty water, so it's not worth the risk. Without hot water, it is going to be tough to clean some dishes. Take advantage of soaking to loosen up stubborn messes. Fill the sink halfway with purified water and wash your dishes. Fill the other sink with just enough water to cover a few dishes. You must conserve water while ensuring your dishes are clean.

Your clothing will need to be as clean as possible to ensure you are not making your body dirty. If you are going to be working outside in the garden or doing something that you know will make you dirty, have a set of clothes set aside purely for those tasks. Put on the dirty clothes to do the work and then bathe and put on clean clothes. You will need to wash clothes by hand. A washing board is great, but if you don't have one (few people do) you can do without. It may not get your clothes as clean as your Maytag, but it will do. Air-dry the clothes either outside or in the house. They will dry, eventually. Develop these habits for yourself and your family now, so that when a grid down event happens, cleanliness will be second nature for you all.

Personal Hygiene

Taking a hot shower in the morning is going to be a bit difficult in a grid down situation. However, you can still maintain basic hygiene. You will want to. No, you will *need* to. You are likely going to be in close quarters with the family and doing more manual labor than you are accustomed to. That means sweating, which can get real stinky, real quick. Daily sponge baths that focus on the problem areas are important. It doesn't take much water to take a quick sponge bath. Start at the top and work your way down.

You could also invest in something known as a camp shower. These lovely tools hold about three gallons water. You place the bag in the sun to heat the water. A nozzle hangs down and gives you a nice spray of warm water. The showers are very inexpensive and a worthy investment for those who want to prepare for a grid failure. Conserve water by getting wet, turn off the water, lather up and then rinse. You can easily take a nice, cleansing shower with two gallons of water. Cleanliness will help evade sickness, will lift your spirits, and will make everyone around you happier.

Cooking/Cooling/Lighting/Heating

When you are holed up in your home with your family, you need to do what you can to keep everybody comfortable. This means cool or warm temps, depending on the season, full bellies, and staying out of the dark as much as possible. This is going to be one of your most challenging tasks. Let's address each one of these issues separately, in order to make it easier to digest.

Cooking

You cannot live on canned beans alone. It would make you ill and very irritable. You will want to build up a nice food storage that will give you some variety. You should be doing this already, if you are prepping at all, so storing food for a grid down scenario will be no different than any other survival situation. Focus on foods with long shelf lives, that pack great nutrition punches into the smallest sizes possible, and make sure to have some variety so that you and your family don't lose your minds eating the same over and over. There are a few options you have to heating up your meals or actually cooking a meal.

• Solar ovens are handy tools you can use whether you have electricity or not. They are a lot like a crackpot. The ovens rely on the sun's rays to heat the box and cook the food inside. You can make your own solar oven out of a cardboard box, tin foil and heavy plastic sheeting. The foil lining will reflect the sun's rays and the plastic sheeting will keep the heat in. You can cook meat, casseroles, breads and so on in your solar oven.

- An open fire is also an option if you have a fire pit or capability to make one. You can use cast iron cookware to cook over the fire. You can also wrap food in tin foil and place it on the hot coals around the edge of the fire. This is one way to make bread, cook potatoes or even a stew inside the foil. Load up on tin foil for your prepping pantry and make sure you and at least one other person are well-versed in starting fires in a variety of situations.

- Coleman stoves are a favorite, but in order to use your stove, you need plenty of propane canisters. There are various opinions about using a propane stove indoors. Technically, you shouldn't. It's a safety hazard. If you can, it's always preferable to cook your meals on the back porch or outside. If inside is the absolute only place you can cook, due to safety, weather, etc., make sure you do it in a well-ventilated room, as far from anything flammable as possible, and take all the necessary safety precautions.

- The barbecue on the back deck is an option. Consider investing in a portable barbecue that uses briquettes and stock up on them. Propane will likely not be available immediately following the failed power grid.

- Sterno cans are another option for heating a can of food or water to use to rehydrate a freeze-dried meal pack. You would need quite a few of these cans if it is more than just you and you are going to be without power for a while.

- If the power failure happens in winter and you have a wood stove you use for heat, you have a cook top right there! You can heat water, cook eggs and even bake a pie on top of your wood stove.

Cooling

If the power goes out in the middle of the summer and the temperatures are skyrocketing, you need to be able to retreat to somewhere cool. If you have plenty of shade trees around your house, you can keep your home fairly comfortable. If you are exposed, you may be better off getting outside and into some shade, as it will often be cooler outdoors in the shade, than inside in a hot, stuffy house.

Keep your house cool by shutting the doors and windows as soon as the temperature starts to warm up. Cover the windows with heavy curtains or blankets to block the sun – you'd be amazed how much just sunlight through a window can heat up a room until it becomes uncomfortable. Open the windows at night to take advantage of the cooler temperatures outside. Dress in cooler clothing. Lightweight fabrics are best and will lift your moods considerably. You can help cool your body temperature by dipping a washcloth or old t-shirt into water and placing it on the back of your neck.

Save the majority of your chores for early morning or late evening when it is coolest out. Hang out in the basement or in the northeast corner of your home that will get the least amount of sun and will therefore be cooler. You can also invest in a solar-powered fan that can create a nice breeze.

Lighting

Although light isn't a necessity to survive, it sure does make you feel better and does make you feel safer. For that reason alone, it's worth taking a look at how you can keep your family in light. You don't have to worry about tripping over stuff and hurting yourself. Your children will feel much safer and happier in light.

Flashlights are great, but do you have enough batteries? LED flashlights are extra great because they are super bright and use very little battery power. Thus, they last for a long time before you have to change batteries, unlike more traditional flashlights. Look into getting a solar-powered lantern or a crank radio/flashlight even. The lantern will be bright enough to light an entire room. This will save you from relying on batteries. Save the flashlight for when you need to run outside to use the bathroom or for more emergency-type of situations.

Another idea is to stock up on emergency candles. These are designed to burn much brighter than the typical scented candles you find at the store. Don't forget candleholders. Spend a few nights with your spouse or children practicing with living by candlelight. This can be a fun activity for the family and in the event of a grid down situation, everyone will feel much more comfortable with the whole idea and practice of living by candlelight at night.

Heating

If the power failure happens during the winter, you need to be able to stay warm. A wood stove is your best option in most climates and situations. Make sure you have plenty of seasoned firewood on hand to burn. It's a good idea to get a wood stove now, if possible, so you can start practicing. It's not that easy to find suitable wood, learn how to chop that wood properly, then learn how to store it properly, and finally, learn how to burn it properly. These are all skills that take time, so the sooner you start learning, the better.

If you don't have a wood stove, pick the smallest room in your house and keep everyone inside. Huddle together with blankets. Body heat will help keep you warm. Much warm than people often realize, in fact. Cover the windows with heavy blankets to block cold air from coming in. If you have a south-facing window, leave it uncovered to take advantage of the heat from the sun. Cover it at night or if the sun is blocked. Dress in several layers. Wear a warm hat. Your body heat escapes through your head. Build a fort out of blankets or set up you tent in the living room. The small space will help trap the heat and will keep you warm.

Many people will have a generator at home. They think that if the power goes out, they'll just turn the generator on and then life will continue like normal. This is a big mistake – especially if the grid goes down in the dead of winter. If you plan on running a generator night and day, that's going to use up an awful lot of gasoline. How much gasoline do you have in storage? Probably not a lot. If you think it will be easy to just rush out and buy some gasoline for your generator when you run out, think again.

It's fine to have a generator and to be prepared to use it, but you'd better have a backup plan for when your generator runs out of gasoline or, worse, breaks completely. You don't want to be unprepared when that eventually happens – and it will!

Conclusion

There are any number of reasons why the power grid might go down. Natural disasters. War. Terrorism. Economic collapse. Governmental action. And on and on. We can't control any of those situations. What we *can* control is how well prepared we will be for them and how we will respond to them. That is the essence of prepping, and prepping for a power grid failure is no different. Yet, for some reason, this seems to be one area of prepping that most folks seem to ignore. Many people plan for wars, government overthrows, extreme weather or, if they're really out there, crazy things like zombie attacks. They don't stop and consider what is one of the most likely causes of a survival scenario: a complete collapse of the power grid and days, months, or even years without electricity. Don't be one of them!

Living without electricity can seem daunting, but if you are prepared, you will get by just fine. You may even learn to appreciate some of the little things in life. You will certainly forge closer bonds with your family members when the technological distractions are removed from your lives. You will learn valuable skills like cooking from scratch and how to build a fire. You would be best served to learn these skill before the grid fails. Talk to your family about what life will be like without power. Do your best to reassure them that you are preparing to ride out the grid failure and they don't have to panic.

Make it an adventure! Learn some camp songs to sing as you sit around your living room in the evening. When you take the time to prepare today, by doing things like storing extra food, water and maybe even collecting extra blankets to add to your linen closet, you are ensuring your family will be taken care of despite the dark world they have been thrust into.

We have seen towns, cities, and even entire states, thrust into chaos following failures of the power grid. Riots, looting, lines at stores and gas stations, and confusion is not uncommon in these situations. Why? Simply because the vast majority of Americans are completely unprepared to live without electricity. It's not something they've ever thought of, and certainly have never practiced or prepared for.

But you are different. You are thinking about it already. You are preparing. You are taking the necessary steps to secure your future and the safety of your family and loved ones. Stay on that path and nothing but good things will come.

Good luck, fellow Preppers!

*****

If you've enjoyed this book, **please** consider leaving a review and letting others know what you thought!

Sign up for Robert's Mailing List to be notified of **New Releases** and **Special Sales**: http://eepurl.com/zvm11

No Spam – he promises!

Other Books by Robert Paine:

Prepper's Pantry: A Survival Food Guide
The Survivalist Cookbook - Recipes for Preppers
Prepping 101: A Beginner's Survival Guide
The Dead Road: The Complete Collection

www.ingramcontent.com/pod-product-compliance
Lightning Source LLC
Chambersburg PA
CBHW060632290526
45793CB00001B/222